Say, Cap!

The New Orleans Views Of Ronnie Virgets

Ronnie Virgets

To Bert :
Best wishes from —
New Orleans —
Ronnie Virgets
1997

Arthur Hardy Enterprises, Inc.

For

The 'Roos: Steph, Mike and Tara

and

Lynne, the perfect duet for me . . .

Published by
Arthur Hardy Enterprises, Inc.
P. O. Box 19500
New Orleans, LA 70179
602 Metairie Road, Suite C
Metairie, LA 70005

ISBN 0-930892-50-X

First Edition — 1997

Illustrations: Lynne Jensen
Art Director: David Johnson
Editor: Don Lee Keith
Typography: Barbara O' Aitken
Lorraine Boudreaux Buchta
Cover Photo: Syndey Byrd

Stories on the following pages were originally published under the title "Razoo" which is
a registered trade name of Firstar Communications of Louisiana, LLP and *Gambit
Weekly:* Pages 18, 24, 26, 37, 40, 51, 54, 57, 66, 69, 72, 81, 84, 87, 90, 93, 98, 103,
106, 109, 112, 128, 131, 136, 139, 142, 150, 153, 155, 174, 182, 185, 194, 198, 204.
Remaining stories reprinted by permission of *The Times-Picayune Publishing Corporation.*
The author thanks both publications for permission to reprint these articles.

INTRODUCTION

"Say, Cap!" was a working-class way of hailing someone, usually a stranger, in the New Orleans of my youth. I think it has the perfect mixture of the elements that make New Orleans such a good place to spend your life on earth: It's breezy and informal, befitting a city where no one stays a stranger long, and yet the shortened version of the honorific "Captain" shows how always we stand ready to show our respect to any person willing to accept it.

It's not used so much these days, like many other good things that are passing away in our time and have passed away in all other times . . . So it's right that we sometimes take note of the things of our time. I hope in some small way that's what this little book does. . . .

REV

The reader should be advised that the book's contents are gleaned from newspaper columns and articles written between the late 1970s and this date. Thus, some of the material will be dated, e.q. using present tense for someone no longer present. Please pardon the inconvenience.

TABLE OF CONTENTS

PROLOGUE

When I was very young, the very old were to be seen on the streets of New Orleans, because the only "homes for the aged" were the ones they happened to be living in. Old men in seersucker pants and pocket watches with long watch chains would find their way in front of the meat market or the barbershop or the dry cleaning store that took horse bets and would tip their hats to the old ladies, come a-shopping with their parasols.

Fierce shoppers they were, too. The butcher would disappear in the cooler where quarter-cows hung from hooks, and then come out and slice. The old ladies would make him hold up the slices against the light and then they'd shake their iron-gray heads: "Too veiny," they'd say. "What else you got today?"

It was one of those old men in seersucker, Mr. Pete, who first convinced me of the magic of Mardi Gras. I'd had my heart set on a costume in the window of this dry goods store, but the day before Mardi Gras somebody else bought it. I went to bed thinking I wouldn't have a costume the next day and cried on my pillow.

The next morning, I went outside and on my porch was a beautiful black felt cowboy hat. I had the launch for a costume, and I remember thinking the hat must have been delivered by an angel whose job it was to make sure everybody masked for Mardi Gras. A week later, my mama said Mr. Pete had found the hat and, thinking it was mine, had tossed it on my porch on his way home at dusk.

Mardi Gras, I'm sure, always colored the way New Orleans kids regarded New Orleans adults. Where else do kids get to see their male role models wearing ballerina skirts and rouged faces, waving Jax or Regal beer bottles and bellowing heavy jokes? We would always walk to town, stopping at the Deutches-Haus or the Druid's Home on Camp Street and being entranced all the way by passing flatbeds of maskers dancing to a jazz of free-sweating combos.

In those days, New Orleans was just an overgrown small town. No matter how far afield you traveled from your neighborhood, somebody knew someone in your family. You'd stop at a distant McKenzie's or K&B, and the lady behind the counter would ask your parent, "Did you ever live near Bayou Road?" or "Are you related to the Mrs. Scramuzza goes to St. Anthony's all the time?" If you were, then you exchanged the age-old New Orleans question: *"How's ya mama?"*

Your own mama was usually busy, doing clothes by hand in sanitary tubs. If you were good, you might be allowed your bath in those sanitary tubs. And she was always trying to make something sweet from leftovers: rice pudding, bread pudding, lost bread.

The diseases that threatened us were both malevolent and mysterious. In the winter, people got grippe and, more ominously, walking pneumonia. In the summer, there was always lots of talk about polio, and keeping kids out of the water. But in this town, kids are never very far from water: in the lake, in the Bayou, in City Park or Audubon Park pools, in the rain-filled gutters or even from the neighbor's garden hoses.

Doctors were called in to witness the diseases only very reluctantly; it was still a town with much faith in less formal cures. In any grocery line, you could hear conversations similar to: *"Nothing that any of them doctors did did my poor sister-in-law any good at all. But this old colored woman . . ."*

Sometimes, no cure worked, and then there were wakes. Funeral homes still had rooms for the close family, so you could spend the night directly above the dearly departed, though not resting nearly as well.

And there was no early retreat from the gravesite, either. You watched the diggers shovel the covering earth over the coffin and often there were some spectacular histrionics by the next-of-kin.

There was a 70-year-old woman who tried to jump on the coffin of her 96-year-old mother, screaming "Mama! If only we'd had a little more time!" Death may come to all, but in New Orleans, we made sure its coming was well-observed.

Because climate used to be more of a problem than criminals, New Orleanians spent a lot of time outside their homes. Mosquitoes permitting, kitchen chairs might be dragged outside for a yard supper under a china-ball tree.

There would be hearing and judgment on the family's business:

here the clan's squabbles were mended, plans made and revised, advice given and gotten on bedwetting or the latest sale at H.G. Hill's store, as the beer and fried chicken or boiled crabs passed from hand to hand.

On summer evenings, the small children would play in the street till about 10 — stickball with electric-taped newspaper for a ball, "dungeons," "Bread-and butter, come to supper!" — while the adults sat on the porches and talked. About 15 minutes before it was time to go inside, the adults would call you over and tell you to cool off "'cause we're going inside in a few minutes." We were never allowed to drink cold water till we'd cooled off because, we were assured, the results were usually fatal.

While we cooled off, we talked about who was the toughest cowboy to roam the cinematic range at the Escorial or the Imperial or the Happy Hour — the adults talked about which nights there were free-dish giveaways at those shows — and Alan "Rocky" Lane and Bob Steele got a lot of votes, though the raw-leather aficionados held out for Lash Larue or Whip Wilson.

But on some golden nights, you'd be taken for a treat: ice cream or nectar sodas or maybe a snowball slogged off a block of ice with a hand scraper. The kids would get permission to "run on ahead" to the next corner, as long as you promised to "get off the banquette when big people are coming." While you waited for slow-moving parents to catch up, you might leapfrog the fire hydrant or debate which members of the jungle kingdom were allies of the Ape-man: "No, no, no! The elephants are Tarzan's friends!"

The really big treats involved in getting in somebody's car and heading off for, say, doughnuts. Maybe at the Verbena Bakery off Gentilly Boulevard, where the family baked them in the basement, or Parkway or Freitag's on South Galvez. Or to a watermelon "stand" — usually picnic tables under sagging strings of light bulbs — where you'd get a slice for a quarter and free salt besides.

Of course, there were vegetable trucks that prowled the neighborhoods, with the vendor yelping "W-a-a-a-ter. . . mel-l-l-ons! Red to the rind!" and your family would buy a whole melon for your birthday. When all the melon had been eaten, there would be a watermelon fight with the remains and you weren't allowed inside until you'd been hosed off in the driveway.

It was on these trips that you became aware of how pungent the smells of the city were: maybe driving past Arnaud's Spice company on Tchoupitoulas, where there might be enough dried pepper in the air to make you sneeze; next the aroma of roasting coffee; then on past Mother's and the lure of fresh biscuits, and a little farther down, the wood-smells of the coffin-making place.

At the French Market, there was Battistella's Fish Market and Buck's Chicken (Buck had made "Believe It Or Not" by killing, plucking and preparing a chicken in less than a minute.) At Bucktown, there was seafood frying.

The males of the families came home from work at the I.C. Railroad or Higgins or Woodward Wight or Dibert-Bancroft and looked forward to a week or two in the summer when they could rent a camp at Little Woods to crab and cook and watch a sailboat drift across the lake's afternoon sun-spill.

If you eavesdropped in the barber shop or Pelican Stadium, or watched them play the pinballs or claw machines at the neighborhood restaurants, you could hear of their male secrets, their *bourree'* games and what the insides of Norma Wallace's or Dora Russo's whorehouses looked like.

But we knew that the males never really ran anything in New Orleans; from Arabi to Avondale, this was a grandma's town.

It was grandma who gave you your first glow-in-the-dark rosary and taught you to make the sign of the cross when your streetcar chugged past a church, and it was she who broke up your childish mock-Communion games (with hosts made from Necco wafers or goldfish food) as "a sacrilege."

But it was grandma, too, who threw salt after a departing salesman or collector so he wouldn't return, grandma who always pulled your bed at least six inches from the wall "so that the cockroaches and the thousandlegs can't climb on your blankets. Them thousandlegs'll get in your ear and make you crazy."

It was grandma who dressed you up to go Easter-shopping at Krauss or MB, grandma who fried up plantains after school, and grandma who warned you not to look directly at the face of the old bag-lady who roamed the neighborhood picking up clothes hangers and old newspapers, "because she's got the bad eye." New Orleans grandmas seemed to grasp these things with a force that no prying modernity could loosen.

Of course we all eventually got older and began to acquire the tricks of making money, the money that would eventually land many of us in split-levels in the suburbs. We'd ride fat Cushman motor-scooters over to City Park and plunder the trees there for branches to sell in front of the church on Palm Sunday or sell pilfered pieces of pipe to Southern Scrap. We got jobs setting pins at Fazio's or Mid-City Bowling Alley, or we served up burgers and delicious root beer at a Frostop, and before you knew it, we were parking at the lake or the Skyvue Drive-in with our dates and eventually marrying one of them for better or worse.

But even now, some of us remember standing in front of sweet-shops for group-sings of "Lil' Liza Jane," knowing we were maybe the fourth generation of New Orleanians to learn the words and tune to that one. And if a good brass band marches by, playing "High Society," our feet start to shift and our bodies start to sway in all the approved second-line fashion.

The essence of such a city blows by me. All I know is that a lot of folks in this town grew up like this, or something close, and I've never met anyone else in the world quite like them.

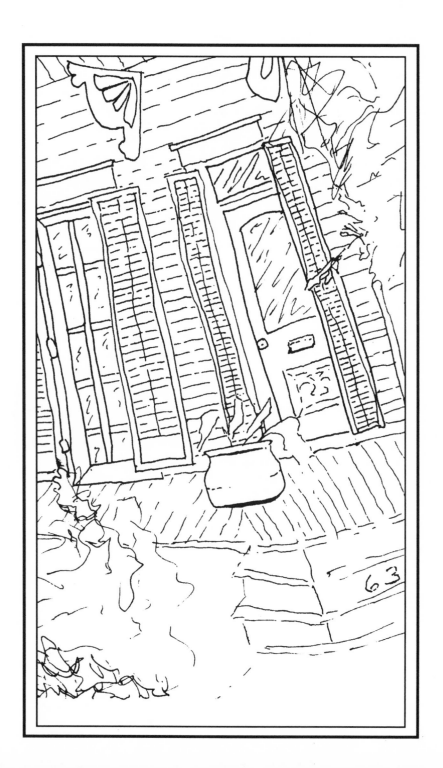

1

All In The Family

"I am the family face;
Flesh perishes, I live on."
Thomas Hardy
Heredity

The bonds are not as tight as they used to be and still ought to be. Especially around New Orleans, where you couldn't go to any Schwegmann's grocery or McKenzie's bakery and not run into a friend of the family. If human history is a tapestry, it's the family that's closest to us in the weave, the ties that bind us to the cloth. It's their stories we tell, their values we echo or repudiate, their lives that give us context . . .

MAGIC LIVES ONE LAST TIME

There had been two children before her, so I knew the warning signs.

"Brenda said there's no Santa Claus, that your parents put out the toys after you're asleep," Tara informed me a couple of Decembers ago. "But she's such a liar."

I looked down at her 8-year-old face as she said it and saw the mix of faith and doubt there. Well. The time had come for my youngest, the time when the magic of Christmas begins to melt from the heat of forced-march maturation.

I remembered when stuttering Jimmy Upton told me there was no Santa, there in the cloakroom of Sacred Heart school. Made me mad enough to push Jimmy Upton against one of the clothes hooks and formed in me an eternal enmity for those who use superior knowledge to make others feel bad.

I said no more to my daughter that day, but I felt once again the sadness of that long-ago moment in the cloakroom. Maybe it was the finality of it all: the last real Christmas for the last child.

By next year, she would realize the accuracy of Brenda's information, would know that the gifts in her life came from hands distinctly human and unmagical. Into each young life must crash a Brenda or a Jimmy Upton.

The next day I decided to make Tara's last childhood Christmas a good one. I made arrangements with her mother to have her to myself on Christmas Eve. I bought a tree for my bachelor apartment and for days stalked the French Quarter shops, buying toys with a definite Victorian look: a little wooden drummer boy, a rocking horse, a porcelain doll, a Santa that resembled a European grandfather.

To make it all work, I arranged for a friend to slip into my apartment after we had gone to midnight Mass and lay out the presents. Let Brenda try to explain how they got there.

Tara and I sipped eggnog and sang off-key carols until it was time to leave for church. She was wearing a red dress and white stockings and had never looked prettier.

I flicked out all but the tree lights, leaving the room bathed in reds and greens and yellows for when we got back.

Mass was long and Tara fell asleep by the Offertory and slid off the pew during the Communion. But after Mass, I knew what to do about her sleepiness.

"It's late," I said cheerfully. "I wouldn't be surprised if Santa has come by my house already. He always gets to the Third Ward pretty early."

I made the drive home a leisurely one, allowing time for the power of suggestion to gather force. "Look over there, Tara! Over that roof! Is that a sled?" After a couple of my sightings, she began to nod wordlessly.

As we pulled up in front of my apartment, Tara caught me by the sleeve. Her eyes had gotten big and they were going to stay big for another hour. "You go up first, daddy," she whispered. "He may be still in there."

We tiptoed up the stairs, me leading by a yard. I flung open the door and gasped dramatically. Tara jumped a foot straight up and then scrambled to my side.

"There they go!" I yelped. "Out the window! Did you see him?"

"Oh yes!" she answered without perjury.

Tara, the family baby, rushed to the tree and fell to her knees. For the final time, she had seen Santa the way he should be seen, and the tree lights played off her unending smile. I memorized the whole scene and knew that I would never again cause such a smile without taking credit for it.

"Ohhh, daddy," she cooed as she peeled the wrapping away from the porcelain doll. "I believe . . . I believe."

For that moment, I believed too; believed in myself and the power of things that yoke us together in belief.

Have yourselves a merry little Christmas.

THE "OLD MAN" AND THE RIGOLETS

Some thoughts at the close of Father's Day, one of the Hallmark company's favorite holidays . . .

The year 1914 was the year when Mr. A. Monteleone erected those wonderful pillars at the entrance to City Park. It was the year Joe DiMaggio was born in San Francisco and Boston's "Miracle Braves" made their miraculous run to the National League pennant.

In 1914, "Birth of a Nation" was produced and Charlie Chaplin made his first movie, "Making a Living." The theme for the Knights of Momus was *Odds and Ends of Nonsense* and Float 11 was entitled "The Monkey's Wedding" and one float later was "The Lugubrious Whing-Wang." And three months later, Europe introduced us to wild combat between whole civilizations in the biggest war the world had ever seen.

It was also the year my old man was born and so in a way was I.

My old man. I can remember the first time calling him that in conversation. It sounded almost like blasphemy, and I remember wondering if the walls, the sky, the air itself would trap the term and whisper it back in his ear that very night. It took a long time before I could say it without self-consciousness, and now that I can, it sounds almost affectionate.

We never really spent enough time together, me and him. In the early years, this was probably his fault. In these later years, it's probably my fault.

There are some things I know about my old man. He was born to a 16-year-old Irish girl and grew up on Gravier Street in poverty and can remember walking down to Charity Hospital where Sister Anastasia, supervisor of the nun's kitchen, would give him some bread or cake to bring home.

His old man was an ice-man with a razor-strap which he applied to children who didn't obey readily enough. When my old man was nine, his old man walked out of the house and didn't come back for another quarter century or so. But I have a hunch my old man loved him anyway, or at least wanted to.

So at the age of nine, he was farmed out to a stern aunt and uncle; when he finished eighth grade, he was sent to work. I don't think he learned much about family warmth there.

Yet he loved to dance, and once I heard this story about him dancing. He had gone to a party uptown where he didn't know many people and there he met a girl from his own neighborhood, a plain and large girl that he asked to dance because he felt a little bad about her wallflower status. He thought that eventually some other guy would cut in — everybody cut in those days — and he could consider his good deed done.

But nobody did cut in, and this plain and large girl had gratefully wrapped her arms about him like he was salvation itself. So he danced with her 14 straight songs. That's one of the kinds of guy he is. . . .

He danced even though he always had a bad ankle, which he said he broke sliding home for the Roosevelt Hotel softball team when he was 20 years old. He bell-hopped at the Roosevelt for some of those Depression years and knows stories about Huey Long and Seymour Weiss and the big bookmakers who used to sit around the lobby in the early evenings.

But he didn't keep that job, and the Depression became very real for him. He still talks of it and how if you're lucky enough to get a good job, you never quit it.

He was lucky to get a good one, working on the river, and he never quit it. It wasn't hard work, but there was plenty of overtime, and since he never drove, it meant lots of late-night streetcar and bus rides to places like the Sty Docks and the Sugar Refinery and the Thalia Street Wharf.

He talked about the Depression, and he had other favorite stories, too. Like about how pirates had kidnapped a youthful Julius Caesar and how Caesar had sworn to come back when he was grown to hang them and had done just that. And how John Wesley Harding had trailed the man who stole his horse from Texas to Canada and killed him.

Stories about guys who didn't take the indignities that most children's old men had to take.

So my old man hadn't seen much great fathering up close, but I remember well two occasions when he did his best and it was good enough. The first was the afternoon I fought Red Kenner. Red was a regular neighborhood terror among us 8-year-olds, and I surprised myself by swinging at him when he grabbed for my Bit O Honey.

Now, in books and movies, this is were the bully turns yellow and gets his lumps. Unfortunately, Red Kenner was tougher than those books and movies and he started whacking me around pretty good. I did get in a wild right, though, that bloodied his nose just as my old man came walking up from work.

My old man knew Red Kenner, "Well, well," was all he said, but he said it proud and put his hand on my shoulder. I thought my heart would bust right through my T-shirt.

The other time was about a year later. He took me fishing at the Rigolets, a rare thing. I was desperate to show myself worthy, but hadn't even caught a catfish all morning.

Then, on the way back, we made a last try under a pier near the launch. It was like a biblical miracle. I began hauling in nice striped bass, one after another. I was wild, caught up in my own glory, while my old man just smiled and took the fish off my hook.

Toward the end of the run, my old man caught one. I panicked. It was my moment, and I wanted to be able to say I'd caught 23 striped bass, not 22. So I pleaded, "Daddy, can I have that one? Is that one mine?"

I guess he could have denied my claim and given me some moral instruction on truth or selfishness. But he looked and he saw there were bigger things involved.

"Sure, baby, it's yours too," was all he said.

That's plenty of what I know about the man, not very much really when you consider the decades of proximity. But that's enough to know, so long as you know the man is your old man because that's one thing in this nutsy world that's never gonna change . . .

GOING AFTER THAT FIRST SQUIRREL

No sooner than he'd reached down to turn off the engine than the son was talking. "Want me to get the guns out the trunk?"

"No, not yet. We'll wait for more light," the father heard himself answer. He lit the day's first cigarette and tossed the pack on the dashboard.

The son sat in silence. Already there was something about the boy's attitude on his first hunt that the father didn't like. Maybe the boy was acting too bored or something; maybe he could hear the boy thinking that things shouldn't take this long to unfold.

The father decided he was being too judgmental. He exhaled a nose full of smoke and watched it gather around the inside of the windshield. Through the smoke he watched the waning moon and thought back to his own first squirrel kill.

The half-moon had not yet quit the sky that long-back morning, and he'd kept seeing it out of the top of his left eye.

That eye was busy, too, because for several minutes it was trying to keep the bird in view.

Later he would not be sure what kind it was, though he would have guessed mockingbird or small jay. At the time he never wondered what kind it was; now he wondered at everything.

Of course the bird had been his ally, had in fact delivered the squirrel up to be killed.

He knew this as it happened, because he knew in his stomach that he didn't know enough about squirrels yet to find and kill one.

He had stopped walking aimlessly and was standing by some bushes under an oak, holding his .410 like a tired sailor holds a mop, when he heard the rustle of leaves and the cry of the bird.

As he looked up, he saw only the bird and the flash of another form and he could feel the gun slipping from between his arm and his chest and falling away to the wet leaves under his feet.

But he never looked at the fall of the gun. He moved slightly to his left so that most of his face, not the eyes, went behind the brush.

The squirrel — not yet seen as a squirrel but only as a phantasm —

must have looked down from the pursuit of the bird and seen the hunter. Or the phantasm of a hunter. The animal immediately froze somewhere in the limb just above the boy-turning-hunter.

He didn't know squirrels yet, but now he knew what to do, how the game would be resolved. It was like hide-and-seek, played between the eight-graders and the lower grades and all the square block was for hiding with only the railing on the church steps as base.

If the eighth-graders could find you, they would give you a red-belly with the flats of their hands or maybe pull your pants off and throw them on the roof of the band room. If you moved from your hiding place, if you grew tired of being cleverer than they, then you were caught.

Just like now. If you move, you were caught.

He kept looking up. This must be the attention to visual detail that a painter has. Seeing things so clear that seeing becomes feeling. Seeing the wind-stirred trees in their rooted minuets, the contour of a limb, the forking of a branch, the breeze-flutter of a leaf, the sun playing off a cobweb . . .

He knew just about where to look. The scene of the squirrel's total muscle-control-for-life act was framed by two branches that came together like a jagged, irregular heart.

He'd been looking almost straight up, and his neck was jammed back into his shoulders and it hurt. To look away would be to lose, of this he was certain. He was amazed at how many noises, how many thoughts, how many fears, tried to tear his eyes from that shapeless frozen squirrel, who was trying to master his heart and his haunches so that he could go on living and being chased by birds.

The betraying bird had seemed to acknowledge the gravity of the hunting human and stopped his chase. After a few minutes, he flew away.

A plane, a single-engined prop plane, flew off to the side of the morning moon, but his eyes saw it only peripherally.

Only when he felt the neck pain winning over his brain did he let himself think of something of the city. He thought of Dorothy Boudin, who always smiled at him from her desk on the next row. He thought of getting this squirrel and bringing it to school and how her face would look when she saw it in his hand.

Then he remembered the gun had to be retrieved. He sank to his knees in the wet leaves, never looking down.

When he stood up, the gun felt cool and good in his hand. Now he felt ready to wait all day, even though his knees were trembling some.

A sneeze began to build inside him, and he felt like every particle of his body was rushing to the middle of his face. But he'd had time to get ready for it; he pinched his nose, bit his lip, resisted the irresistible. After a while, his eyes filled with water, something went down his throat, and the sneeze went away quietly.

When the squirrel finally moved, he showed only what looked like a yellow belly, big and old, as he sprang to a limb below.

There was a place to shoot, but he felt proud that he had outwaited an animal wise in maturity. He would gamble now, waiting for the easy shot when the big squirrel stopped moving and if that wait cost him the shot, so be it. It was the wait that mattered more than the shot, and he had won the wait already . . .

The squirrel did stop finally, about 15 feet from where he'd broken from cover. This time the boy hunter never lost sight of him and killed him at the edge of the branch.

He picked up his first dead squirrel and put him in his coat pocket. Like every other moment of love in his life, he felt good and he felt bad. The squirrel had his eyes shut tight like he was sleeping and was a real beauty.

Now, my Beauty, I'm coming back with my sons to hunt your son, and good luck to us both . . .

"Are you ready to learn how to hunt squirrels?" he suddenly asked his son. The boy nodded, half-sure that's what he wanted. "Come on," the father said. "It'll be a good day. Not much wind."

The father stepped from the car and made the sign of the cross as the boy was getting out the other door. The boy saw him do it and smiled one of those young smiles that has no understanding whatsoever in it . . .

A TALE OF MEN AND THE SEA

He heard the generator kick on and the brothers, one short and one tall, move to the nets on the pier at the front of the camp. He had only a few minutes now to lie there, wanting to get up and wanting more sleep, only a few minutes before the old men, the old fishers of men, began their wheezing search in the dark for shoes and trousers and then cursed their way to the commode.

The fingers of light gripping the hallway next to the dormitory-sized bedroom told him that some of the old men had reached the long kitchen. Soon some of them would be producing the warm smells of biscuits and bacon, while others clattered among the whiskey bottles atop the icebox, seeking the day's first cough treatment. Phlegm-cutters, they called these first drinks.

He made his way to the long dining table, poured some coffee and lighted a cigarette. It was his first time at this fishing camp, this place that belonged to his father's friends, perched in creaking dignity on California Bay outside of Empire. Across the table sat his father and son. They had come to this camp together many times and the younger man had learned many good things here.

Now he was along, glad for his chance to be away from rooms of fluorescent lights and men who tied their luck to the insides of briefcases.

Glad, too, for the chance to maybe work out some of those generational things between men, things like hierarchies, deferences and debts. Things that are so tough to work out when one wears his youth like armor, the other wears his experience the same way and the third is stuck uncomfortable in the middle.

Across the table, his son sopped up the last egg yellow with a biscuit and looked up brightly. "Well, Pops," he said jauntily, "I guess we'll see who the best fisherman is today, huh? Think my dad can keep up with us, Pa-pa?"

The boy's grandfather looked at them with eyes of bored superiority, like those of a circus leopard. "Your daddy never could fish," the old man said.

Aw no, he thought. Let's not spoil it on something so stupidly masculine as this.

A half-hour later the three of them were anchored off a spit of prairie grass, baiting their hooks and watching the new sun yawn across the marsh. It was windy and bracing and he liked being in the middle of the boat, with his father on one end and his son on the other. It was like looking backward and forward at yourself, he thought.

They all fished on even terms for 20 minutes. Then the boy's pole bent hard and his reel whined under the strain of what was clearly a big fish.

He glanced sideways at the boy struggling with the fish, saw the way he pursed his lips and squinted his eyes, the way his mother did when she concentrated on something. He thought of the boy's mother, now a thousand ideas and one divorce paper away, and caught the melody of her: The Temptations' "My Girl," one of those old songs of finger-popping hope. The boy looked like her, all right.

The pole bent even more, the angled line made another circle and bolt. The boy yelped, squealed something about "Go ahead, you bastard! You ain't going anywhere!"

He turned and looked at his father, grinning, in the bow. Only during the struggle with a fish would the old man have grinned at the obscenity.

"I guess maybe he's the best, huh?" he asked his father, glad to yield.

"It's no contest," the old man said happily, grinning into the wind.

The boy may have his mother's face, he thought, but he's got my sound, his father's noise. The thought gave him comfort as he missed a trout's strike once and then again on the retrieve.

FATHER OF THE BRIDE

Each sunk warm and deep into the back seat, they had talked in the twenty minutes it took the limo to get to the church. At a traffic light, some children in the next car had looked in at her and waved. He remembered that much.

The rest of the time they had certainly talked, but already the only thing he could remember was the children waving.

Now he got out of the limo and walked to open her door because that's what the photographer wanted and up till now, the photographer was running the evening.

She came out of the limo's darkness like a large white dream. He blinked and tried to look at her at this moment as a stranger might, in order to remember it better later, but he could not.

There were people waiting on the church steps and he wanted the distraction of them, but only for a moment. He shook hands gladly and hurriedly.

Then they stood in the back of the church, while people bustled over to say How Lovely. He tried to stay busy smoothing down the front of his shirt.

He looked down the aisle at the faraway altar. It looked much the same as the day of his First Communion four decades ago. No. It had looked holier then.

She had chosen this church even though she had no connection to it and he was glad because he had all connection to it. He had been an altar boy here, pulling black cassocks out of a mothball-smelling closet, swiping at the dust on his shoes with a handkerchief. Marching down the aisle, swinging the censor that billowed incense, trying to catch the eye of little girls he knew. Sitting on the altar under a thousand solemn eyes, his face happily burning with importance.

Could the anticipation of this day ever flit across his mind then? Or even five years ago? Ridiculous. How could these things, these things of mass importance, stay hidden from us for so long, he wondered . . .

Suddenly there was a flurry of anxiety in front of him. The six-year-old flower girl had to go to the bathroom. Someone grabbed the little girl up and was gone.

He shut his eyes and tried to call to mind all he could of the beautiful young woman next to him. Could he remember clearly what she had looked like when she was six? He cursed himself that he could not.   But he remembered some things, some poor and wonderful things. He had been overseas when she was born and he remembered that first maternity-ward-window photograph of her and the dozens of Polaroids that came for the next eight months, each making her both more and less real.

And he remembered too the day she had fallen off her bike going down a hill at City Park and the tender and terrified way he had wiped at her blood with lagoon water. . . .

There were more memories coming now that there was not time for them. He turned to her and said, "I love you, baby," and kissed her.

Now the organ began to hit triumphant notes. "It's our turn, Pops," she said. She tried to say it with lightness, but couldn't quite pull it off. The words slapped softly against his back like a wet shirt. "Let's do it," he heard himself say and instantly recalled it was what Gary Gilmore had said to the firing squad.

He began to walk, he could not help it. It was a big church, and it seemed like he had to walk endlessly before he could make out the faces of anyone in the pews.

For many steps, the altar seemed to be retreating from him in slide-projector blinks. His heart was walking around in his chest in new shoes and he could feel his tongue and teeth playing games. He wondered how far away some tears were hiding . . .

Then they were at the altar. He felt the weight of her presence next to him, a weight he'd once fled, now wished for because of its elusiveness. He tipped that weight, let it go. And then he was lost and was glad he'd said, "I love you" in the back, because now he could say nothing. He kissed her cheek, and guided her right hand into that of the nice-looking young man waiting there.

They turned from him and he was alone. He was glad there were only a few steps to the pew.

He watched the ceremony unfold and thought back to the days when he'd been an altar boy at weddings. Days before air-conditioning, when almost every ceremony had someone fainting. His back would be to them, and he would hear the collapse, the crumple of silk and taffeta. . . .

Look at them together, he thought. What did she know of him or he of her? Now she would be a wife, and she was already looking enveloped in a wifely cocoon, already taking on a wifely glaze.

Were they trying for so much, these two? A marriage, a happy marriage. As simple as a drink that will still any future thirst. River is deep, river is wide, uncertain milk, uncertain honey, on the other side. . . .

The priest urged that every night they say to one another, "I love you. I really do." And then the vows and rings were traded and she and he had become official answerers to love's constant call and all its secret things and dominions that can never be known by a mere father of the bride.

Near the end of the ceremony, the flower girl slipped into his pew with tears rolling down her cheeks. What was wrong? "Stephie's going away," the flower girl said piteously. "No she's not," he lied softly.

Now it was over and the bride and groom turned from the altar and flowed away from him. He stood up and smoothed his shirt-front one more time.

Never would she be closer than today. Of that he was sure. And never would she be further away than today.

Of that he was hopeful. . . .

2

Sinn Fein: Ourselves Alone

---

*"All good things which exist
are the fruits of originality."*
John Stuart Mill
On Liberty

No other American sub-group thinks they are more original than New Orleanians. More singular, too. More discerning, savvy. Our rivers and roller coasters are better than yours. Our ice is probably colder than yours, and if it isn't, we make better use of it — Sazeracs and snowballs, for instance. We are like Texans or New Yorkers about all this, except our bragging is softer and usually reserved for ourselves alone. . . .

A TALE OF TWO NEW ORLEANS WORLDS

It's only 16 blocks. Just a straight shot down Washington Avenue.

In New Orleans, that's all there is sometimes between two worlds that can't excuse each other.

Gloria walked the 16 blocks.

She walked on Washington from South Claiborne Avenue. She passed the bars — Club Rhythm, Lee's Treat, Shadowland Bar and Hotel, Big Man's Super Game Room. She passed the Baptist churches, too — Willing Worker, My Redeemer, Guiding Light, Shiloh. Between the bars and the churches, the houses leaned toward each other like tired old friends.

Then, for a few short blocks on each side of St. Charles Avenue, Washington bursts out of its blight. There, and on the side streets, people with "My Cat Loves Me" stickers on their Volvos live on soft sofas beneath brass-trimmed ceiling fans.

One of these people, a young Uptown Lady, was tending her lawn the Sunday afternoon when Gloria, who was very pregnant, padded up and asked for a glass of water.

With some reluctance, the Uptown Lady invited Gloria inside. Gloria's eyes got very big when they saw how the woman lived.

"Ohhh. This is a big house," the woman remembers Gloria saying. "Is that a pool out there?"

"I was embarrassed," the woman said later. "But Gloria didn't seem mad about the differences in the way we live, any more than I'm envious about Buckingham Palace. I don't even think about it."

Drinking the glass of water, Gloria told the Uptown Lady how she lived. She was one of 14 children raised in three bedrooms in Kenner. This was her eighth child coming, and she was only 21. None of the fathers ever came around.

Furthermore, she and the seven babies were going to be evicted from their two-room apartment in a few days because some thug had stolen her welfare check. She couldn't tread water any more. So she had taken the 16-block walk, looking for somebody nice in this nice neighborhood.

The Uptown Lady was somebody nice. She came up with most of Gloria's rent-money, and made a few calls and got someone from Catholic Charities to take Gloria on a shopping trip to Schwegmann's.

Back at her sullen apartment after Schwegmann's, Gloria sat down heavily while her boyfriend and the woman from Catholic Charities headed for the kitchen to put the groceries away.

"We met over at Shakespeare Park," she said. "This one comin' ain't his baby, but if he finds a job, he's gonna be the daddy to all these eight babies!" And over Gloria's somber face flashed a smile, quick as a fingerpop and lasting about that long. . . .

There were only two babies in the apartment, Gloria said, because the others were with a neighbor. Both are girls, plump and exuberant. One of the babies wandered under the table, and Gloria called to her with mock severity: "Gimme a lick of that candy, girl!" She got a lick, gave a hug in return and then folded her arms across the table and put her head on them.

There is a dreamy passivity, a childishness, about Gloria. She shows no remorse or anger about being cared for by others.

When the woman from Catholic Charities got up to leave, she asked Gloria if she was going to have her tubes tied after the baby was born.

Gloria nodded yes, but after the woman was gone, she said, "If I had it to do all over, I'd had 'em all. All eight of 'em. Maybe they'd take care of me when I get old."

Later that night, the Uptown Lady got a collect call from a pay phone. It was Gloria. She had a chance to buy a hot color television, and all she needed was $45. She said with the new TV, she could watch her stories in color.

The Uptown Lady didn't feel quite right about it. But she wiped off her lipstick, took off her jewelry, got in the family Mercedes and drove down Washington Avenue, hoping that nobody would jump in her car at a stop-light.

When she got to the corner of Claiborne, Gloria was standing there. The Uptown Lady rolled the window down and pressed the $45 into Gloria's hand. Gloria said she'd better keep the Mercedes moving, so Uptown Lady made a couple of left turns and drove the 16 blocks back home.

This is the way things turned out: Over the next few days, the woman from Catholic Charities checked and found that the welfare office listed Gloria with two kids, not seven. She went back to Gloria's apartment and found the same two babies. The boyfriend was there with a couple of buddies, sitting around smoking a reefer.

Meanwhile, the Uptown Lady found that another woman in her neighborhood had been approached by Gloria the week before, and she, too had given her money for a color TV.

The next time Gloria phoned, the Uptown Lady said she believed Gloria had lied to her and she wasn't going to give her any more money. Gloria just said, "Well, OK," and hung up.

The Uptown Lady later told friends she knew she had been duped, but she didn't regret what she'd done because, two kids or seven, Gloria was in need and probably had spent a good part of her life lying to people wealthier than she.

When it was all over, nobody was too happy with the way it ended. On the other hand, they seemed pretty much at peace with their consciences.

A LOOSE REIN ON THE FACTS

The eighth-floor restaurant at the Meridien Hotel, right by the pool, has taken to giving the names of jazz greats to its entrees. Right here, the spinach quiche with fruit trimmings? It says ask for the "Bessie Smith."

"Is this the same Bessie Smith who sang 'Gimmie a Pigfoot and a Bottle of Beer'?" I ask the attendant. He didn't know. Disgusted, I decided to walk the French Quarter in search of historical integrity.

Hey, how's about taking one of those mule-drawn buggy tours of the Quarters? To see ourselves as others are told to see us. Every quest for authenticity has to start somewhere.

My buggy of choice was to be shared with a couple of couples from Norwich, Conn., and drawn by a mule named Ira, I believe. Ira's driver, The Major, displayed an impressive number of gold teeth and an elegance of expression not heard since Jerry Lewis was young.

Ira took off. Clipclop, clipclop, clipclop. "Now there is the Presbytere," The Major informed us. "On the second floor there, Napoleon and Thomas Jefferson met to sign the Louisiana Purchase, 17 states for $15 million."

(Hmmm. I always thought Napoleon's only appearance here was on dessert menus. As for Jefferson, I thought him too much a rationalist to come to New Orleans for any reason, even a good real estate deal. But wait . . .)

Clipclop, clipclop. "And when Jean Lafitte wasn't black-smithing, he had letters of marque from Madrid that enabled him to take after all the Spanish treasure ships."

(Wow. No wonder the Spanish Empire self-destructed.)

On we drove, The Major taking time to shill for a couple of neighborhood restaurants where prices are higher than a cat's back. "Now this is the Flea Market, where internationally famous artists bring their wares every weekend."

(Yeah. All the way from Norco and Gentilly. Ugh! Quite a pothole there, Ira. Our streets were planned by Gilbert D. Julie, a Sorbonne engineer who, I'm sure, owned a small garage specializing in front-end work.)

The Major kept referring to the Sieur de Iberville and the Sieur de Bienville as "The LeMoyne brothers," making them sound like proprietors of a waterbed store. "They came attracted by our oysters and pearls and by our gold and silver mines," The Major added when he thought no one was listening.

Clipclop, clipclop. "Now this is Esplanade. On your left is the French Quarter. And on your right is the NON-French Quarter," our guide intoned.

Finally we got to something that interested the Connecticut couples, who'd seemed very blase' about Napoleon. "On that balcony is where Elvis Presley stood in *King Creole* and sang 'Blue Bayou.'" The Connecticut ladies aaahhhed, even though I remembered the song as being "Crawfish." Maybe The Major meant to say the crawfish were caught in Blue Bayou.

"And on the right is the Cornstalk Hotel, where Elvis stayed before he was famous," continued The Major, certain he now knew what we craved.

"What about Marie Laveau?" asked a Connecticut lady. "I'm glad you asked that, because she lived right there," The Major said. "She was bought at an octaroon ball by Jean Lafitte and of course, died a nun in the old Ursuline Convent."

I felt like a stranger in my native land as I got off the buggy, patting Ira. Most days you can find a pleasant time in New Orleans. Finding some historical integrity may take a little longer.

A STREETCAR NAMED MAJESTIC

The real beauty of a streetcar ride begins with its noise.

It starts with a sound like water running in another room. Then more metallic, then the rolling sound, finally a flat diminishment until the brakes lock in steel-shrieking, bone-rasping halt.

"Step up, please. All the way into the car."

Workday quittin' time. Everyone's underwear and charitable impulses are damp. A bunch of schoolboys have been waiting at the stop, playing "Not It" around some chained-together police barricades. The fat boy keeps yelling "Time out!" just as he's about to be tagged. Get in — come on, boys. You shoulda had your fares ready.

That fat boy sprawls on the seat next to a lady in a flowered dress, purple necklace and matching purse, doing a crossword puzzle in ball point on the window ledge. Ding-ding. We're off again.

Picking up speed. The car, shell for the homeward-bound, moves with confined abandonment, swaying soft then hard then soft again, a reactionary rhumba. The passengers, sitting or standing, pick up the rhythm of the drive, their heads full of undirected thought: Play, work, music, quiet, self, others, heaven, hell, all borne on Timken Made-in-U.S.A. shocks.

To ride the St. Charles line from a window seat is to move inside a cyclorama of the city's sociology. Past the dirty-windowed bars between Poydras and Lee Circle, men in stocking caps standing outside temporary-manpower offices. Close your eyes, sway with the motion a few minutes, and open them to see silver-haired, golden-coiffed ladies who say "How won-durr-ful!" a lot, walking their little dogs past mansions.

The car screeches extra loud going around Lee Circle, coasts to a stop across from the St. Charles Tavern, a never-close place where cabbies hang out. On the back wall of the tavern, a green-neoned streetcar winks out at the real thing. New passengers, slow to get on. "Step lively, folks!"

The new passengers are a man with a wart on his chin, a woman with skin too old and eyes too blue for the tan she's carrying around. They have a visitor's curiosity and they speak to one another in low tones about what they are feeling and seeing. . . .

How did they first see the streetcars? Old, certainly, but not antiquated like the trolleys in Charleston or San Francisco. Still proudly pragmatic, a blue-collar sweeper through the silk-stocking district, a district with both changes and immutables, the streetcar somehow perfectly balanced between the was and will-be.

Going fast again. Past churches and banks, houses whose late-Minoan colors flash by like a palette. The tourists, the wart-man and the tan-woman, look hurriedly at the houses. The houses, big, fine houses, sit empty of striving, just quietly proud to be a part of it all. The greatest part of a city should be grand. You find your-self hoping the tourists are impressed . . .

All along the Avenue, the oaks have yellow ribbons nicely bowed around their throats. Trees that drank rain before there was mechanical warfare are now dressed up for a war with laser beams.

Many of the houses, plain and fancy, bear flags, almost evenly divided between pagan and patriotic, Mardi Gras and American. Between Second and Third streets, flying from houses across the street from one another, large purple-and-gold flags, the kind that signal Carnival royalty, look across the Avenue in silent social salute.

The street signs flash by: Foucher, Marengo, Duffossat. In the little park at the corner of Octavia, maids or sensitive men push per-fect children on swings. At the next stop, the crossword-puzzle lady gets off after first ringing the ancient electric-cord signal — bzzzt bzzzt. — and the tourist couple crane their necks toward a house they find interesting. The car rocks and the neutral-ground bushes brush its windows. "Please Keep Head & Arms Inside the Car," the sign reads.

At some point, the bare bulbs on the car ceiling blink on, light-ing the interior like a boarding-house bedroom. The light seems to signal something to the four schoolboys who'd been playing "Not It" at the car stop. Rambunctious again, they spill to the front of the car and take up positions behind the driver . . .

Like a century of children before them, the schoolboys spread their feet wide, try to stay stationary, no hands, through the street-car's stops and starts. When they are lurched from their spot, they reel into one another with exaggerated force and slap each other's backs. The streetcar is the city boy's reply to horses. . . .

In the old days, the streetcar drivers all had leather-encased watches that they hung from a nail, beautiful old watches that gave a sense of order to a ride that always seemed safe yet adventurous.

Even without watches, the drivers stay busy, producing the bbr-rrt, bbrrrt of the throttle, both hands working, pumping the foot-pedal bell against encroaching automobiles. When one streetcar driver passes another headed in the opposite direction, they still give cool fraternal waves and smiles, unable, unwilling to hide the boy-joy of being in command of something so grand.

Screech around the riverbend at Carrollton. Stop on Willow, a block from the streetcar barn, and then moving again, stopping less often, picking up power, heading for the end of the line. Raise or lower the notched windows, the pull shades, feel the rumblings under the floor and realize you're riding the kind of thing that makes you feel you can just jump on it and go anywhere . . .

End of the line. But for these streetcars in this town there is not, should never be, a real end of the line. In a few minutes, the car begins to rumble up Carrollton again. It bucks and jumps at first, blue-green electric sparks slashing along the overhead lines.

The tourist couple, the man with the wart, the woman with the tan, have stayed aboard, switched seats to the neutral-ground side. The car is almost empty now, so they feel free to talk and laugh more, commoners in the king's chair, on tour of the Avenue . . .

MUSICAL REVERIE

A friend thinks Saddam should be forced to watch a taped Twins-Mariners doubleheader every afternoon. A good punishment as it goes, which is not far enough. Throw in the tape of a full Grammy Awards presentation, and we're talking some serious retribution. . . .

Yet a few weeks back I found myself flipping the channel-changer back to the Grammys again and again, compelled to see if one the homeboys, Wynton or Gatemouth or Harry Jr. or Dr. John, would show the world that the long, stormy and sweet romance between New Orleans and music is alive and a notch better than, well . . .

Who can match the music of this town? Satchelmouth and Slow Drag, Mr. Jelly Lord, Johnny and Baby Dodds, Big Eye and the Fat Man. Pete Fountain and Jimmy Noone, Booker and 'Fess. The Brothers Marsalis, Neville, Prima and Assunto, the Shields brothers, the Brunies brothers and the Boswell sisters. Snooks and K-Doe. Al Hirt and Allen Toussaint and Alphonse Picou. Did ever a place this size make music that size?

What causes it, other than the natural receptivity, the necessary laziness, of the people who grow up here? Artists have long noted the climate here and the mysterious effect it has on the play of light. Perhaps it has similar effects on the travel of sound. Or maybe it's because this was never a factory town or even a commercial town, and the air had the liberty and room for much joyous noise. . . .

Whatever the cause, music has layered and layered here for so long as to make osmosis, and osmosis makes music-lovers and music-lovers, even if they can't tune a ukulele, make for musicians . . .

And, of course, the live bands. Somehow even the little off-key combos that would enliven some little dance at the Druid's Home on Camp Street or the Deutsches-Haus carried magic in their instrument cases for me, a magic that clouded over their worn faces and jackets. Red-faced adults trodding happily if not rhythmically on the wooden floors, with us kids, finally permitted to see the celebratory side of our elders, moving belt-level among the dancers to get closer to the bandstand, to see where "Tipperary" was coming from . . .

And live bands on trucks for Mardi Gras, not in any parade, but a truck simply hired to drive around town, with the hirees getting out at various bars or neutral grounds and dancing to the music they'd brought along with them.

From my boyhood I remember one group stopping on "the greens," on Jefferson Davis Parkway, nearly dusk, and watching the tired dancers move slowly as the drummer dragged his wire brushes across his cymbals. How I wanted to join in the dance, be part of the music! One red-cheeked woman in a blue clown suit must have known, because when her male clown companion collapsed in mock exhaustion against the side of the truck, she summoned me over to finish the dance. I could tell she was looking over my head and smiling conspiratorially at her beer-guzzling date, but I didn't care. I remember wanting the song to never end, straining my ears to catch each upcoming note and praying it would have no hint of finality to it.

My face was buried in the bow on the front of her costume and it made my nose itch, but sometimes, when we turned, I could feel her breast against my cheek and feel it move when she giggled. I was in love, all right. . . .

I was always in love with the drums, too, even though there were many instruments whose music I preferred. The drums just seemed to be in mild-mannered control, walking languidly across the cymbals to "Moonglow," the noises floating to me along the sidewalk from the Banks Street Social and Carnival Club or where the WeDK or the Beachcombers were throwing a soiree.

And, too, I could hear the air-brought drum-sounds from the upstairs back bedroom, my bedroom, with the boxing pictures pasted all over the walls. Saturday night dances at Sacred Heart a block away, the drums carrying the music along from old O'Brien Hall, murmuring promises that one day soon I would be old enough to pass the scrutiny of Father Fay at the foot of the steps and go upstairs, up to where the music played. . . .

In the meantime, you pedaled your bike to the Quarters, bringing along the shoeshine box because that way you could stand longer in front of places and hear George Girard or Sam Butera, Sharkey Bonano cupping his brown derby over his cornet, Lizzie Miles singing "My name is Lizzie from New Orleans and I sure do like my rice and beans . . . I'm a salty dog!" and some 12-year-old trumpet prodigy named Warren Luening, pumping out the fast notes of "That's a Plenty" at Tony Almerico's Parisian Room.

Sad to say, none of it rubbed me enough to be able to make music. Once the man who delivered Luzianne coffee door-to-door carved me a flute out of a piece of sugarcane stalk. That's about as far as I got. . . .

But I still keep a wooden flute around the house and sometimes I'll pop on a record by George Lewis or Sidney Bechet and pick up that wooden flute and turn it into an E-flat or soprano. Puffed cheeks, stung lungs, clumsy finger-flights over the air-holes, noodling and wailing with the band, their sounds generously swallowing up my alkaline tones, and we're all making New Orleans music together. . . .

Last week, I applied for a loan from People's Bank of Arabi. The manager's name was Tony Manalla and we weren't three minutes into my checkered financial past before were talking about music. About how he's played clarinet and alto in little weekend combos for years. He said one night Pete Fountain was in the audience and during the break, Pete came over to put his arm around his shoulder and said "Boy, you do nice work!" and how that was the best Tony Manalla had felt in his life. . . .

I didn't get the loan — many would have turned it down — but I knew what Tony felt about us and our music. Conscious, somewhere, somehow, of the main current, having a perception of what Eliot described as "not only the pastness of past, but of its presence." This town's gonna produce a lot more Grammy winners, and me and Tony and a whole bunch of you are gonna be part of it.

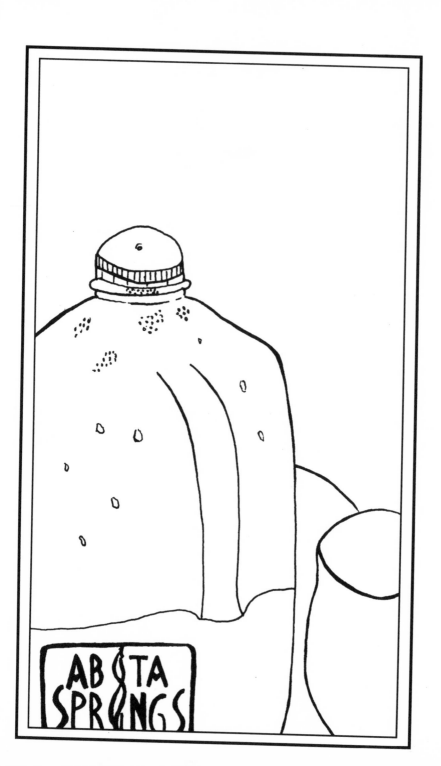

3
Water

*". . . no verse can give pleasure
for long, nor last, that is written
by drinkers of water."*
Horace

Everyone knows New Orleans is in a mildew saucer, with a river on one side, a lake on the other, rain over our heads and swamp under our feet. We do everything with this water but drink it. . . .

BORN ON THE BAYOU

It was in fact the birth cord of the city itself, a pathway discovered by the Sieur de Bienville, a connection between the lake and the river, winding past cypress forests, marsh prairies and reed breaks to the place that would mark the boundary of New Orleans.

In those early years, it was fed by Bayou Metairie and Bayou Gentilly, and it spread four fingers into different parts of town. It became an important commercial artery into New Orleans from Biloxi and Mobile, and from her house on Moss Street, the wife of Mayor James Pitot would send her cook down to the water's edge to buy oysters and game and spices from the procession of market boats.

But there were always laws higher than the laws of commerce being practiced on its shores. The legends tell of the Indian chief Waw-hewawa discovering the trysting of his daughter Owaisee and the Spanish soldier Sancho Pablo under the oaks near its mouth, and killing the Spaniard. There were lurid tales of voodoo rites performed by Marie Latour and her followers, rites attended by some of New Orleans' most respectable citizens.

Then too, there were the years of recreation on it. The mile-long pier extending out into Lake Pontchartrain, the hotels and houseboats, the carousel whose carved horses ended up in City Park. And the bandstands and beer gardens, the places where Oscar Wilde lectured and William Thackeray and General Grant dined. Tranchina's, Leonard's Casino, Noy's and the Over the Rhine restaurant.

Civilization and the centuries have chopped hard at it. The Metairie and Gentilly bayous have silted up until they are nothing but the front lagoon in City Park and ponds alongside Greenwood Cemetery or Dillard University. No longer does Bayou St. John proudly roll to the city's boundary; it now dies a trashy death at the foot of a brake-tag station. These days, it is crossed by 10 brooding bridges and a sleepless interstate. Its shores are besieged by a Space Age condominium near Harrison Avenue and a dreary high-rise apartment near Esplanade. Somewhere between them is a city housing project.

The voodoo gods who were once beseeched from its shores seem to have floated off to more serene places.

Those are ways that history and commerce look at Bayou St. John. There are other ways.

There was a long time when the only history I knew of Bayou St. John was that my renegade grandfather had once spent two decades in a houseboat on it and my father had caught his first fish there, and so, in my turn, did I. I never knew for sure, but I guessed that all three of us had swum naked in it.

I knew the bayou as a backdrop for living history, a place of urban fantasy that was rarely far away from the many rental houses of my childhood, a place to go. "Wherya goin' after school?" "Goin' by the bayou."

My first fish. Can't remember if I was using for bait the wetted innards of French bread from Parkway Bakery or worms dug from alongside the old cleaners, but there was the much-imagined, yet still unexpected tug-down of the cork, the triumphant raising, the goggle-eye dangling, stupefied that he could be caught by such a beginner.

The day I skipped school and Tommie Miguez and I were standing on opposite shores, sailing little wooden sailboats back and forth and Father Fay drove by, and stopped and got out and caught us. I learned the lesson of fear.

And another lesson, on another day I was to skip, and sail the bayou with some friends on a homemade raft we'd built. But I couldn't get away from school, and the raft turned over, and a boy we called Fu Manchu swam to safety, but another boy named James Lay and another boy whose name I can't remember got tangled up in seaweed or something and drowned. It was in all the papers.

Still more things to be learned. One Saturday, hiking all the way over to DeSaix Boulevard to take a girl named Patricia Finney fishing. She was a pretty girl with big eyes, and her momma fixed us sandwiches. We went by the DeSaix Bridge and I caught a few red-bellied perch and Patricia Finney's big eyes got even bigger. Impressing females was never so easy, or ever so impressive, again.

And the freedom of the bicycle! Hauling ass down Marconi,

T-shirts knotted around our waists, then hopping the fence by the park driving range to shag a few re-saleable golf balls. Cutting over to the bayou to cut down some Roso cane and sharpening the ends to points and trying to spear garfish from one of the bridges, swatting at one another with cattails plucked from the shoreline, whooping and free as wild Papuan boys.

For many of my time and place, first beers and cigarettes were entertained on the bayou after dark. Cigarettes, three-for-a-nickel Philip Morrises from the corner grocery; beers from Bizot's Bienville Beer Garden, bottles of Jax, drunk through straws for maximum power. All purchases made "for my mama" or "for my daddy." Naturally enough, there was a night when two Jaxes and two Philip Morrises on an empty stomach pitched me right off the Dumaine bridge. The bayou was being drained that summer, giving us a Goya-esque look at stumps dangling lost hooks and corks and me a very bad smell from landing in a fetid little pool next to one of the stumps.

And there were the bridges to swing or jump from. The Moss Street bridge was used to hide under and look up passing skirts. There was the time Raymond saw his aunt coming and pleaded with us in whispers to refrain this once, but Raymond lacked muscle and so, therefore, did his argument. The old Black Bridge, swinging on a rope. And the highest, the scariest, the Lakeshore Drive bridge by the old Coast Guard station, leaving your insides fluttering up to choke off your Tarzan yell and whether you hit the water hard or clean, you got out smiling and headed to the top again.

The morning chill got you running past the American Can Company on your way to serve 6 o'clock Mass. Then you'd hit the bayou and your eyes would catch the play of the sun's golden ax on the water and your face would start to warm up. And your foot would hit the wet shore grasses, and up they would come with a hum, a hundred landing on each hand and another hundred on your face. And as you sprinted out of the grass, away from the bayou, swatting at new mosquitoes, you were smiling because you knew the mosquitoes meant the approach of summer and days when you could hang by the bayou all day long if you wanted.

So much for the childish things, when we all saw as if through a glass darkly. Why do I still find myself on the bayou's banks now?

If there is an innate unity to Bayou St. John today, an emblem of its repose and dignity, it is likely in the crook that begins just past the Pitot House and extends down to the Dumaine bridge. In the winter, especially, it seems like a fresh-washed green sheet spread to the sun, waters lapping against its cement sides and rusty bridge underpinnings, going-south ducks bobbing regally in its middle.

Just past the Moss Street bridge, the bayou seems to cradle Holy Rosary Church, with its long-limbed oaks softening the face of institutional religion, rising to dominate the landscape until, rising still higher, they are dominated in turn by the church's copper dome.

Mass is over, and the parishioners spill onto the sidewalk and begin their walk, lovely and dignified, home. The old ladies, shiny in Sunday dresses, open their parasols to keep the sun from their slackening shoulders. Here one walks a step or two ahead of her husband or brother and talks over her shoulder of the parish priest's reaction to some matter or another. Her companion, who moves like someone who knows how to be out and about in wool and not sweat, nods but does not answer.

His eyes stay glued on the woman's back where, from somewhere under her flower-print dress, a laminated scapular of the Madonna and child atop pink roses has escaped to give public testimony to the old woman's private adornments. The old couple move through the dark, cool archway of Holy Rosary's school, out to the warm and sunny glare of Moss Street, twisted follower of the bayou's course.

I walk behind the old couple until they turn off at Bell Street, and I keep going along the bank, wondering if I can still get hot jelly doughnuts at Parkway Bakery. Here and there, I pass large-hatted fishermen, enduring without hurry or apparent concern their largely futile quest as one suspects fishers of the bayou have always done.

I notice they are almost all very young or very old. Is there any better blending of the idealism of youth and the acceptance of age than the fisherman? He deserves more than any of us his eccentricities and exaggerations, because he pays for them uncomplainingly with his time and he above all others knows some of the secrets of that time's passage and of its fickle shifts between ally and enemy.

And the bayou, with its unthreatening flow, is a riverine minuet, a perfect tempo for the very young and very old. Here, only a few yards from gracious homes, is the perfect city place for shaking off the city.

Near the Orleans Avenue bridge, I watch two little boys. One is fishing, and the other is throwing pebbles at the first one's cork. The one fishing is getting red in the face.

I think back a decade, and my own son walking toward me with his first fish, caught in the bayou by Old Spanish Fort. It was a crummy little lake catfish, caught on a piece of baloney from our lunch bag. He was walking toward me, classic frieze, with his bowl-shaped haircut and kindergarten T-shirt, holding that cat up like it was covered with rubies and gold. I hope one day he will have a son he can bring to Old Spanish Fort and have that kid land a crummy little catfish. Then my son will know the sound of a father's heart when it really starts to sing.

So now I'm getting near Parkway Bakery, near the bayou's end, and then I think back to a story my father told me maybe a dozen times over the course of my life. When my father was an adolescent, he was walking the bayou banks when an old fisherman with watery blue eyes happened to slide his cane pole back. My father tripped over the pole, and the old fisherman advised him to watch where he was going. My father responded with a youthful curse. "And then," is how he always finishes up the story, "that old man looked me right in the face with those watery blue eyes and very softly, 'Remember, sonny. You're going to be an old man someday, too.'"

That pristine lesson has stayed in my family for more than 60 years now, and I think I'll always go back to Bayou St. John until I can pass it on to somebody's grandchild. Bayou St. John is a good place to be young, and I have a strong hunch that it's not a bad place to be old, either.

CROSSING OLE MAN RIVER

The trip begins with a long and loud engine shudder, portending something massive about to happen — and why not?

This is, after all, the Mississippi River we'll be crossing, the closest thing to a myth-river this side of the Nile. And not the Mississippi River from the rarefied air atop the Crescent City Connection (the only bridge that sounds like it was named for a Chalmette dance team), where it looks like a long sheet of the brown paper butchers use to wrap pork chops.

No, here from any of the decks of the Canal Street ferry, twenty five-cents cheap, the river looks alive and moving. Out there in the middle, the "Full Moon River" glides by with no crew in sight. A ghost freighter, riding high in the water, going where? Been where? And moving downriver, the "Mare Lodf;" is that pretty red flag on the stern Norwegian?

What a river. Unless you've entombed your imagination in an unmarked grave, this river will find it and put it back to work. Check out those sparrows taking off from the trees of the open-sky West Bank, headed for the bustling towers of the East; how far can the far shore seem to a sparrow's wings?

There are other things to see on weekday mornings on the ferry, things to be seen in the crack-of-dawn faces of people going to town to make or spend money.

The bicycle riders get on board first, soon after the ferry's deck hands have tied up to the gouged-wood wharf on the Algiers side. The deck hands wear bright orange jump suits and do their jobs with the cool elan of those in service to a machine that is watched and depended upon. They seem to know the bike riders and wave and talk to them.

Two riders on this trip: a white teenaged girl with a satchel of schoolbooks and hair dyed as lavender as her pants; a black teenaged boy dressed in a bus-boy's white shirt and dark bow tie. After them, the auto traffic clanks aboard.

On the second deck, the pedestrian commuters come on in a

throng and begin to disperse. Some will stay indoors, but in good weather this makes no sense. The breeze is best on the top deck, but you can actually see more from the second deck.

Like a wonderful mix of faces-of-the-city: Blue-blazer guys and gals who will soon be speaking in complete sentences until the end of the work-day, brushing against the wrinkled-pants guys and the women with the grim assignment of loving them.

A young woman blows on her freshly-done fingernails and reads from a blue pamphlet. The pamphlet tells her how to get a fair reading from the state welfare's Office of Eligibility Determination. The reading makes her frown.

Outside, a tugboat of a man, cheerful and bouncy-tough, walks along the rail and looks around for a stranger who'll listen to what shape he thinks the world's in this morning. Finding none, he puts his elbows on the rail, his chin into his hands and stares at the river.

Who knows how atypical his thoughts? You can only see what he sees, smell what he smells: the legless dogcloud overhead, hanging limp from its own rain; the late-burning French Quarter streetlights, clinging to their cathode life; the aroma of restaurant cooking drifting out from the bank . . . Whatever he's thinking, it makes him smile.

It could be anything bringing on that smile, anything in the perfect commuter trip, five minutes in the open air, the final five before facing hours of commerce and congestion, churning across a myth before having to do the Reality Rag.

On the way back to Algiers though, you remember that a couple of weeks ago a man with "Sylvia" tattooed on his right arm dove off this ferry and wasn't fished up until four days later. Yes, you could see the Mississippi having that effect too, could imagine something in the river calling you to jump, to make your final capitulation here.

The rush hour is over now and it is easy to take note of a passenger who is traveling back and forth. He is a black man, old and neat, a man wearing the sadness of lost health and a pair of beautifully-shined shoes. Oxbloods.

Straps from the life jackets stored overhead flap and clink in the breeze. The man doesn't notice, doesn't move from his seat, only stares at the West Bank, coming and going, He looks like a man with few wishes left, and maybe this is one of them.

The ferryboat captain, who's really good at his job, noses his craft into the far end of the pier and lets the stern come slowly around. The deck hands in the orange jump-suits tie and open the liftgates to the next round of bikes and cars.

Castoff. The trip begins with a long and loud engine-shudder, portending something massive about to happen. . . .

On the second deck, the old man with the beautifully-shined shoes hunches his shoulders as the world beneath him begins to move and waits for the next five-minute refuge, twenty-five cents cheap, from the considerable amount of things a man won't reveal even to himself.

VENUS RISING FROM THE GULF

It was a splendiferous day, a God-given day. But before I went out to greet it, I flipped off the MTV channel, where they're televising Spring Break these days.

In my salad days, there were no Spring Break institutions. For most folks around New Orleans, there was only the Gulf Coast.

Ronnie Two and Buster had trip money from their weekend Reserve drills. Ronnie Two was in the Marines, Buster in the Navy. The service was like a private code between them, something to keep psychic distance between their 18-year-old selves and the 16-year-old selves of me and Nick.

Nick was one of the neighborhood's better *bourree'* players and he'd been putting trip money aside here and there. I got mine throwing papers.

In those days, you delivered papers in the morning and collected for them in the afternoons, or weekends, or whenever you could pressure customers into coming up with forty five-cents.

So I collected hard for a week. Some people would come to the door and say come back next week. Or, I don't have it because I thought you only collected on Saturdays. Some would leave the door open. And down the shotgun house you could see them counting up the coins from on top the refrigerator or out of a coin purse. If they brought back two quarters or a half-dollar, you would fumble around and say you only had pennies, hoping for that nickel tip. Some would get tired of standing in the door and say, "Keep the change," but others would just wait till you fished up the five pennies. In those days, a lot of people felt like that about a nickel.

Nick and Buster went over to the Coast a day early in Nick's aunt's tan Studebaker. Me and Ronnie Two followed the next day. We made our way to Powers Junction and started thumbing. Bingo! Three chicks in a Ford sunliner ragtop. Me and Ronnie Two in the back seat. Ronnie Two is showing the chicks his "Devil Dog" tattoo. I cannot think of a single complete sentence to say, but the hair of the girl in front of me is fluttering in the wind and I take it in my hands. Her over-the-shoulder look starts out friendly, but ends differently. I let go her hair.

Ronnie Two is talking away, but suddenly he leans back and says, louder than the wind, "Wouldn't want to be a hoe!" Hoe is how he says it. "Hoes got a problem!" As soon as they could stop, the girls put us out. We hitched the rest of the way to Mississippi with an old guy who drove a pickup for the county.

The sequences of the week are a little cloudy now. There was, of course, some he-ing and she-ing going on, ducks and drakes, boars and sows, coursing with the pack. In our minds, and our minds only, we were sexual predators. Everyone else must have seen us as carrion crows, always on the edge of the real action, hoping for leftovers.

There were some high-born ladies from a Catholic girls' school out on a pier one night, but a chaperone with a flashlight showed up and ran us off. Another night, we snuck into the Edgewater Hotel and played a little strip poker with some Gentilly girls, but the house detective broke that up before midnight. There was a bonfire on the beach one night, but all the girls were too interested in a guitarist singing "Scotch and Soda" in a Mississippi stumpjumper accent. Another night, Nick and I went to the Star theater in Bay St. Louis to see *The Blob* because Ronnie Two and Buster had dates. Afterward, Ronnie Two bragged they'd done the deed, but Buster avoided our eyes, so we guessed they'd got nothing.

Mostly, we just drove the Studebaker up and down the coast highway, sipping on Schwegmann's beer from home. Discount Magic.

The last night, we slept on the beach again and woke with the sun. She was walking up from the water. Venus Rising from the Gulf, her bronzed skin covered with wet sand, her white two-piece suit skimpier than anything this side of the French Riviera. Her stomach was flat and there was roundness everywhere you wanted roundness. She was a movie star and we were stagehands.

Only, she looked crazy and moved crazy and talked crazy. Ronnie Two took her by the hand, talking trash, and heading her for the motel just across the highway.

The rest of us held back, talking, hoping. "She must be smoking muggles." "Naw, she's on goofballs." "Think Ronnie can get a room?" "Think he can get her in a room?" Ronnie Two came out of the office with a key. He took her inside a room.

The rests of us scampered to the back of the motel, trying to peep through the jalousied windows, whispering, giggling. "What they doing?" "Think we'll get to do something?" An old guy fooling with the lawn sprinkler system kept eyeing us, so we walked out front.

Then the door flew open and she came running out the room. And as she ran, I heard a shapeless cry leap from my throat, as it did from the others. Then with the others, I began to curse her and our collective luck. But somewhere down inside, way too far down to find voice, I found myself cheering her getaway.

Goddesses, even crazed goddesses, should never consent to be groped by carrion crows in a Mississippi motel. It makes them mortal and to be mortal is to be forgettable.

Since that time there have been many places visited that were more glamorous, but few as romantic. There have been encounters with other women, too, not all of whom ran away.

The arithmetic of a life now totals thousands of half-slept nights, the sum of which dims the details, even the existence, of most of those places and those people. Them, I can't see anymore.

But that image of the stoned Easter goddess, running bronzed and beautiful across the highway, wild hair streaming behind? Her I can see right now. With 16-year-old eyesight, hard and clear . . .

An Afternoon's Shower

The natural history of a single rain shower . . .

It started out hard, drops jumping up from the asphalt like silver crowns, and within 10, 20 seconds, freedom of movement was gone.

The people on the uptown side of Canal Street stared at the downtown side. Canal Street seems to widen, does widen, when it's raining and you don't want to get wet.

For a couple of minutes, nobody moved. Then the first umbrellas appeared, bobbing timidly down the street with the hard rain splashing off them like white fountains. It's funny to watch umbrellas on the move, so comical in their feeble brand of hubris. It is amazing how battered some umbrellas can be. The prettiest were the big ones with "Whitney Bank" stamped in red letters on their tops.

There were differences among the umbrella people. Some seemed to smile a gloating smile at the absent-minded and gamblers caught without protection. But more just scrunched down, grimacing in their dryness, and walked with the head-down, eyes-up look.

Most people didn't move. They huddled under alcoves and awnings and began to mentally weigh time against comfort. Better to arrive late or sopping? A thousand suppers and a hundred seductions hung in the air, which was slowly beginning to smell rainsweet.

If the hard rain had kept up a few more minutes, it surely would have begun to gnaw deeply into many moods. But suddenly it eased, falling straight down, making soft overlapping circles on the sidewalk, running off umbrellas in pearly drops. A tease of a rain.

The slackening forced the people under alcoves and awnings to become falcons or rabbits. The falcons, knowing the world belongs to the movers, moved. The rabbits, knowing good things come to the waiters, waited.

A young black woman in tight slacks held a *Louisiana Weekly* newspaper over her head and headed across Carondolet. There she encountered New Orleanians driving in the rain. Drivers, too, fall into classes: Either they concede nothing to the weather or they concede everything. The driver in the blue delivery truck conceded nothing, and his speed through puddles sloshed heavy water onto the woman's tight slacks. She shook her newspaper at him.

From the front edge of Pennison's Hair Design, a young man with a tourist knapsack leaned out to catch some drizzle in his cupped hands. Then he leaned out more to catch some on his tongue and threw back his head to laugh. Now rainwatching is a solitary thing, and rain makes you feel alone. But the people around him smiled in understanding. Who can resist the charm of someone, anyone, singing in the rain?

It began to fall hard again, rain pellets springing up like minstrel dancers. A middle-aged businessman crossing Canal Street during the slack got caught in the middle. He refused to hurry now and tried to look impervious, but the new water cloaking his eyeglasses made that difficult.

Under the awning at Hansell-Petetin's, a little girl looked crestfallen that her grandmother had failed to move them before the hard rain started again. The little girl had more time than anyone, but of course didn't know it; she knew only that weather changes adult plans. "We won't go to Jesuits church; the next time it slows, we'll go right to the store for your dress," grandma assured.

It slowed in another 10 minutes or so. Now it fell lightly, like a priest sprinkling the congregation at Benediction. A woman in open-toed red heels smoked a Salem and said to a small tan woman: "I only come down for the sales. I just wanted to get some of them pantihose, two for five dollars."

"I wanted to get me some shoes for about twenty dollars, but they had nothing in my style in my size," the small tan woman said.

The other woman puffed on her Salem and pondered the legacy of New Orleans showers on a summer afternoon.

"I wonder if this is gonna make it more hotter?" she asked between puffs.

4

Never Rains
On Our Parade

"What was he doing,
the great god Pan,
Down in the reeds by the river?"
Elizabeth Barrett Browning
A Musical Instrument

New Orleans is passionate about its religion, as are many places with a residue of paganism. Every nation needs a sandbox, a place to play, and New Orleans is more than willing to shoulder the role — impromptu parades have right-of-way on city streets. The pipes of Pan (half-god, half-goat) are often heard and heeded here. On several occasions, I have heard them myself. . . .

ROAD LIGHTS ARE ALL GREEN

On the gravestone of novelist Nelson Algren is chiseled this final advice: "The End is Nothing. The Road is All."

The road today is straight down Severn Avenue, then left on Metairie Road, all the way to the railroad tracks. Our marching club will be in the middle of a two-mile green ribbon that will snake and stomp its way through tens of thousands of well-wishers.

St. Patrick's parade. Ersatz religious commemoration. Great community theater.

Waiting to start at the assembly area, the club members jig, sweat, toss down foamy beers and slap one another's palms. We are glad to be together again. In and out of luck, we return year after year for this, a little fatter, a little grayer, always reaching a little further back for one of our best days and cheering each other on until we grasp one.

The floats, the derbies, the socks and suspenders — everything to be seen in the assembly area is green, the color of hope. Illuminated by the spring sun, the promise is there that each marcher can suspend the split in himself. The split whereby sometimes the head rules, sometimes the body. But on bright afternoons like this, one says to the other, "Hey, let's do this thing together!"

OK, let's do it. We're rolling, falling in between our beer truck and our sound truck. The sound truck is playing street-jazzy versions of things like "Down by the Riverside," "Didn't He Ramble" and "What a Friend We Have in Jesus," the gathering thunder of a brass-band bass drum introducing each tune.

People are there to cheer, to buy some of what we're selling this day. People of all ages and complexions who want some connection with the Irish, a conquered people who've somehow remained conquistadores of the spirit.

Young men are hardly to be seen. But their sisters and girl friends are, some blushing buds, some exploding pods, all wanting to be noticed.

And the old, too. Women swaying and clapping. Did they wait until they shriveled to take a chance on feeling good? And the men, mixing gingerly and vehement movements with their brittle pelvises and tricky hips. They, too, knew this tempo, still know it.

But the mechanics of proper parading draw a line between them and us. The paper flowers, beads and doubloons we throw are for them. The cane dancing is for us. You shake your flower cane, you whirl it, you slow-drag it along the street like Fred Astaire in *Top Hat.* This dance, coarsely rhythmic and colorfully macabre, is for you, you and your club comrades. Together you strut, sashay and rubberleg in a joyful, bouncing act of defiance of life's probabilities: This is the heart of parade marching.

Onto Metairie Road. The beer is having its effect and then some. Ankles ache, knees start to lock, but you keep dancing because parades celebrate a victory over tiredness. Paper-pushers and lawn-tenders, grub-worm slayers and yea-sayers, whether your life is as empty as a winter tree or you have your very own everything, you have need of such victories.

Because for all of us, there are too many days when the weight of the world's stupidity and our own intolerance of it are too much to shoulder. Days when you just have to tell anybody who'll listen: "I'm so tired, baby, I could cry. I'm so tired, baby, I could die." That's when it's time to parade.

Outside Metairie Tavern, I'm cane-dancing feverishly when an old man with teeth as dirty as his cap grabs my arm and says, "Take it easy, man. We all gonna end up in a hole in the ground."

"Hey man," I tell him back. "It's the way there that counts. And this is a great way there."

"What a Friend We Have in Jesus" bubbles from the sound truck.

KREWE BREWS A WILD TIME

It's no place for the heavy-hearted, Whitey's Seafood and Billiard Center on Downman Road, on the first Saturday of Carnival season.

That's the day the Krewe of Crawfish stages its annual Mardi Gras parade. Indoors.

This is the time of year when New Orleans shows a slice of itself that is unfathomable to many. What's happening is more than a drain on the public treasury, more than a ritual enactment of the privileged caste lording it over the rest of us.

It's also the time when the whole town cries for something beyond the ordinary. When folks paint their faces, forget their bosses and live on a keener level for two weeks of glorious excess.

The folks who gathered at Whitey's for the 13th annual Krewe of Crawfish parade last Saturday were at that level.

Parades and krewes, of course, mock pomp and royalty. The Krewe of Crawfish mocks the mockery.

It's almost 2:30 in the afternoon and the joint's been jumping since 10 a.m. The four pool tables are covered and whole families are devouring sacks of crawfish. The combo is wailing and the folding chairs of the "reviewing stand" are full. Behind the bar, right next to the Miller tap, Queen Debbie King adjusts her tiara.

Boo-Boo Aucoin, 86 and sporting a gray porkpie and brown tie, says he's here because "it's a good place to meet beautiful women." A few of the younger guys are break dancing, but 300-pound Louie Gueldner glides blithefully by, his arms around an ingenue several years his senior and a few pounds his junior. Kids scamper between wobbly adult legs. Johnny "Papa-San" Owen looks around and crows, "This is a real New Orleans party!"

In the krewe den (nee kitchen), Maureen Morrale is applying makeup. Hulking Doug Carlos is having a face painted on his stomach, red lips around a cigarette-clutching navel; an over-sized stovepipe hat with a brim that rests on the shoulders will complete the persona of a "Big Jelly Blow Belly," of which Carlos is assuredly one.

Costumes for the celebration hang unwashed in Whitey's storeroom year-round, and sometimes fit the wearer. This year's throws and beads are courtesy of Icarius, a defunct Carnival krewe.

The crawfishers mount the five decorated dollies that serve as floats. The king is Whitey's crusty bartender, Larry Luthi. He says the coronation is the best thing that's happened since he got married. Ronnie Theriot climbs on the throne of the "Commode Float" and wonders why "grown men behave like this."

For some reason, they do. Parade leader Freddy Tauzier, 84, announces the start by pushing his cheeks together to produce a braying sound. Out from the den roll the floats, pushed by "mules," a group of such stalwarts as Chauncy "It's-Soft-But-Not-Stale" Malcolm, Wilson "Shuck-Em-All-Day" Theriot and Danny "I-Needed-The-Time-Off" Fasnacht.

The joy is unconfined. Floats are pushed into spectators' legs. Doubloons bounce off walls and quick kisses earn cheap beads. King Crawfish XIII, looking at least as regal as those lop-earred boys of the British royal family, toasts his queen with Thunderbird wine and brags, "We're the only parade that's never rained out!"

This is Carnival at its core: Folly chasing Death around the Wheel of Time. Folks are singing, swaying and shouting happy exaggerations above the music with no thought of trusses, torpid livers or unmet mortgages.

There will be an Easter this year and a Thanksgiving and a Christmas before the Krewe of Crawfish rolls again; there will be wakes and weddings and baptisms. But for the Whitey's crowd, those are just some things that happen between parades.

A PARADE DOWNER

It was a great night for parading. The Friday skies were clear and the lights of the colors of Mardi Gras atop the Hibernia Bank invited everyone to the Krewe of Hermes.

There weren't all that many people around Lee Circle when the first floats arrived. Hardly enough to make necessary the carny-looking food trailers that served candy apples and sausages with onions and peppers which tasted wonderful in the chill of the early evening. But those who were there seemed glad they'd come.

"An old-fashioned parade," a young man said approvingly as the king's float rolled past, drawn by hooded and blanketed mules.

There were a lot of out-of-town bands, including one full of bagpipers from Canada, and they all looked great emerging from the cavernous dark of the overhead Pontchartrain Expressway. "California! Whoo-eee!"

"Minnesota! Yeah, thanks for coming!" the thin crowd yelled.

Here came the rows of flambeaux carriers — can Carnival actually be considering their abolition? — the Druidic aspect of their libertine glow contrasting splendidly with the straight-legged discipline of the Marine Corps bands they surrounded.

An appreciative rolled-up dollar skittered into their path. The first flambeaux carrier didn't spot it, but the one right behind him did and scooped it. Then he turned his face to the crowd, wanting to acknowledge the thrower. His face met yours and he grinned and raised his fist in salute and you did the same.

Another Carnival-caused connection with a stranger. You see it all the time. People scrambling savagely for a pair of long beads and then handing them over to a nearby stranger's long-faced kid. You don't even have to use the verbal bridge ("Where y'at?" "How ya doing?") you usually have to toss across the social chasm that happens when you meet a stranger on the trail. It's Carnival and it has a language rich in wordlessness for dealing with strangers.

Float riders know the language well. When you put on a mask, you make yourself a stranger to everybody. On these floats, reflecting in the big windows of the Tivoli Towers, the riders in their masks looked like lurid, gargoyled figures out of the old Prince Valiant comic strip. They were throwing enough trinkets to keep the thin crowd happy.

"Boy, know what I'd like to do someday?" a young man in the crowd said between floats. "Go to Carnival in Rio. Man, they have body counts for their Carnival!" He talked about the samba clubs dancing themselves to death and other aspects of the risk of fun.

Minutes later, float 13, entitled "A Royal Wedding," was rumbling slowly past the front of the Tivoli Towers when the driver jammed on the brakes. He looked over his shoulder and flapped his arms in despair.

The driver got down and walked on the neutral ground side of the float. Three cops who'd been standing on the corner unsheathed their nightsticks and began moving toward the stopped float.

"Somebody fell off the float," somebody in the crowd said.

"Every year something like this happens. Or a little kid gets caught under a float," somebody else said.

The cops gathered around the fallen rider so that all you could see from the curb were his bright satiny pants and beige-looking boots. He didn't seem to be moving at all.

Then the cops began moving everyone back. The rest of the riders on the neutral ground side of float 13 motioned with their arms for everyone to get back.

The riders all looked stunned. You could see only their eyes through the masks, but that was enough.

A cop yelled up to ask if anything had come out of the crowd. No, several riders shook their heads. Had he complained about anything, the cop yelled up.

"No," said a rider from the very front of the float. "He was sick and he was sitting down. Then he just slid over the side."

The cop asked something about wearing a safety belt and the nearest riders shrugged.

Two middle-aged ladies with Midwestern accents said they had seen the fall. "He went right over, just like that. He seemed very relaxed. He didn't put his arms out or anything."

Now the fallen rider was unmasked. Two paramedics had

arrived and taken off his mask and cut his satiny tunic in half, and people in the crowd, strangers and all, were connecting with this man.

"He's probably got a wife and family waiting at Gallier Hall and they're not even gonna know something happened."

"Some little kid's gonna be waiting to catch a lotta stuff from his daddy or paw-paw."

"At least he went like a New Orleanian oughta."

The ambulance got there quickly. When they wheeled him away, the rider was on his back. They had immobilized his neck and he wasn't moving. "Holy Mother of God," a young woman said.

Then, as it had to, the parade began to move.

Nobody in front of the parade knew what happened and the people in back knew something had happened, but not what. Only we in this little half-block knew, had marked this awful thing.

The riders on the last floats kept jiggling and throwing, and after a minute or so, people in the crowd began lifting their hands to catch.

The last float passed and then there was only the siren and flashing red light of the trailing fire truck. A young couple stood on the neutral ground. She kept looking down St. Charles Avenue. "Whatsa matter?" he asked.

"I just don't want to read the papers tomorrow," was all she said.

THE OYSTER GIRL

"Honi soit qui mal y pense." (Evil to he who thinks evil of me.)
Lydia Thompson, America's first burlesque queen, circa 1870

"The beauty of it all ended," Kitty West says wistfully. "They were getting their music from a juke box!" More than three decades cannot mute the disbelief in her voice.

Burlesque raced across American culture like a high-speed passenger train and, like the passenger train itself, was enchanting in its youth. Salomes in closed-reefed corsets, can-can, cootch, shimmy, finally the strip-tease, the peep show writ large. No longer all-girl revues; now a single girl and her dance, a *pas de deux* between her body and a spectator's gaze.

Like passenger trains, whose life spans it paralleled, burlesque offered a splendid view from the club car bringing up the rear. In New Orleans, that would have been Bourbon Street, from the end of World War II to the dawning of the Age of Aquarius. Kitty West was in that club car. . . .

In those days, Bourbon was known to locals simply as "The Street" and it was a fine place for burlesque to throw its own farewell party. In places like Gunga Den, the 500 Club, Ciro's, The Sho-Bar and Stormy's Casino Royale, you could even catch echoes of Olde Vaudeville. Every program had stand up comedians like Shecky Green and novelty acts like Phil D'Rey and his Talking Ape. ("Why are you in uniform?" / "I'm starting a gorilla war.")

But the true headliners were the girls. In that subtler, if not gentler, time they were known as "exotic dancers," and if there wasn't true exoticism, there was a kitsch that was even better.

Like teacher-turned-stripper Patti White, "The Schoolboys' Delight." And Alouette, who could do centrifugal and counter-centrifugal twirlings of her tassels. And Evelyn West, "The Treasure Chest," supposedly insured for $50,000 by Lloyds of London. One act featured a woman "caught" in a roped web while a male "spider" crawled over and peeled away her clothing.

As big as any on The Street in those golden-sunset days was

Kitty West, though few knew her by that name. To rooms full of smooth and excited people, she was simply "Evangeline the Oyster Girl." Four times a night, six nights a week, a throbbing clarinet wail would summon open a giant oyster shell, and a beautiful young woman would emerge in a flowing white gown — and flowing green hair.

"It was supposed to be seaweed," Kitty says with a raspy laugh. "It was peroxide, vegetable dye and I don't know what else. Once it poisoned my roots and I had to have my head shaved."

Green hair and disrobing while dancing with a large plexiglass pearl was typical of an exotic dancer. So, perhaps, was Kitty's route to becoming one. . . .

"I was always the school kid who wanted to be in the front of the room," she remembers in a voice rich with reverberation. "I'd try to teach the other kids to dance and they'd laugh at me."

That would have been in tiny Shuqualak (pronounced "sugar-lock"), Mississippi. "We'd go to town in a buggy because we were poor, poor, poor. I worked in an ice cream parlor to pay for dance lessons. Elaine Dennery and I would play dress-up and my mama would sing. 'A jewel in heaven, a jewel on earth.' That was my name: Abbie Jewel Slawson."

In 1947, Mama's 17-year-old jewel answered the beck and call of bright lights and big city. "Someone took me to Gasper Gulotta's, where Miss Hurricane was head lining. She had some sort of seizure and I went on for her. Taking my clothes off! My grandpaw was a minister and I kept seeing his face beyond the lights."

Two weeks later, Abbie Slawson was Evangeline, a role she would play in four-inch heels for the next 13-plus years. Don Ameche came to see her and so did Cesar Romero and Sinatra. She made *Life* magazine and sometimes $1,500 a week. Offstage she wore furs and gloves and turned away Stage Door Johnnies by telling them, "Oh, you've got something better waiting at home for you."

So did she. She married jockey Jerry West and two sons followed. And the business on Bourbon began to change: less choreography, more gynecology. "I never even wore a G-string," Kitty says proudly. "If you had an act, a presentation, you didn't need to pull your clothes off."

So she walked away from the footlights and fat checks to raise a family. She's not the sort to make herself old by looking at each day as a pale echo of a day gone by, yet, "I still sing and dance around the house, and I've still got all my furs and dresses in a closet, though I never wear 'em because you don't wear furs to church."

Today's Bourbon Street performances? For the Oyster Girl, it's anti-dancing done to non-music. "It's go-go, wrapping around a pole. No act."

For the last 10 "glorious" years, she's worked as a receptionist-manager for the John Jay salon in the Lake Forest Shopping Center. The salon phone rings. Something about a wash and curling irons for someone who wants to be in front of the room. "That's $19.95, honey."

She hangs up. "Those girls on Bourbon now, they not only can't dance — they can't even walk like a stripper."

My money says The Oyster Girl, with or without furs, could still do both. . . .

BUZZARD BAIT

Early on this Mardi Gras mornings, in the manner of the past hundred Mardi Gras morning, they will come rolling down Laurel and Tchoupitoulas and Arabella and Dufossat and Bordeaux, like some fearless Bacchic force of nature.

And the sleepy-eyed people along these blocks will tumble out of their houses and get down to the curb and the cry will go up "The Buzzards are coming! The Buzzards are coming! Here come the Buzzards!"

And the cry will echo and re-echo down the halls of history, back past such socially-exalted Carnival organizations as Athenians, Atlanteans, Mystic and Harlequins, back past the days of permits and police-planned parade routes, back to a group made for parading when all you did was get a band (Papa Jack Laine or the Excelsior Brass), playing "Over the Garden Wall" and those 6/8 marches and go . . .

Back to 1890 and the first time the Jefferson City Buzzards left the nest.

A tiny history lesson: At the time of the Civil War, Toledano Street marked the upper boundary of the city of New Orleans. Beyond that, to Joseph Street, the area was known as Jefferson City and remained so-called by the locals long after incorporation.

In 1889 a few young neighborhood bucks headed by William Markel and the three Simpson brothers hired a couple of wagons for Mardi Gras and rolled around calling themselves "The Muddy Graws."

The following year, they hustled up about 40 members to meetings at the Markel family chicken house and decided to imitate a couple of marching clubs called the French Market Buzzards and the Phunny Phorty Phellows.

There must have been giants who strode the streets of New Orleans in those days. That first year, the Jefferson City Buzzards hit the streets of the city as cigar-smoking pickaninnies at 7 a.m. and didn't stop until thirteen hours and twenty-plus miles later.

In a 1948 interview, original member Lee Simpson was asked

what were the aims and purposes of the organization when it was founded. The question was asked with as much gravity as if FDR was being queried about the reasons for the United Nations.

"Well," the oldest Buzzard replied solemnly. "Our aim and objective was to have a good time and that is something we never failed to do."

That kind of failure was never in the club vocabulary. Now there have been many a marching group come and gone — or stayed — since 1890: Half-Fast, Lamplighters, Corner Club, Lyons Carnival Club, Garden District Carnival Club. But the peripatetic funsters of the Buzzards have done it longer and harder than anybody and their collective sense of street comedy has always had Mardi Gras devotees wondering, "What will the Buzzards do this year?"

One year, they paraded as scarlet-suited bunny rabbits, with crinolined mammies, bustled madames and a hack drawn by a mournful mule bringing up the rear. Another year they went as cannibals, "and scared one little boy into fits," remembers an old-timer. The cannibals pulled a little cart with a little dog in it, wearing a sign that said "Dog Soup Today." *National Lampoon*, eat your heart out.

And always the parade made its refreshment stops, some two dozen, scheduled and unscheduled, at houses private and public, like Bill Bailey's, Frankie and Johnny's, Fump and Manny's, Grit's, Munster's, the Jackpot Bar, Bultmann's, the Engle Brothers' place on Napoleon and Magazine.

On most recent Wednesday nights at the Roost, plans are being made for more of the same and more on this year's centennial march.

(The Roost, at 5215 Annunciation, has been the Buzzard headquarters since 1907. It speaks well of past and present Buzzard boisterousness. It is a dingy-wall hall, with linoleum floors and the ghosts of Saturday night poker games Joe Schweitzer ran for the club. At his request, Schweitzer was buried with a deck of cards.)

At this meeting, Buzzard president Clarence Lundgren, vice-president A.J. Marshall and Captain Kit LaGrange are trying to impose some parade laws on what is an essentially lawless bunch.

"Remember, no obscene dolls or any of that crap," Lundgren warns.

(It is a difficult thing to maintain the fine line between being happy and being a Hun, but the Buzzards try hard. One grand marshal had his brother-in-law evicted from the parade. One year, the grand marshal himself was evicted.)

The club's "shyster lawyer" John Weigel tells three new members, "You're now in the oldest, grandest and not the most genteel of all Carnival marching clubs. So no cursing on the route. Except each other."

The Buzzards are much in demand to march in parades around the city, but it is their male-only soiree on Mardi Gras day that causes the most friction.

"When my kids were small, one of them said to me, as Carnival got close, 'Oh Daddy. It's about time for Mama to get mad again!" says club historian George Luft. "But I told her I was a Buzzard before I married her." Since 1949, Luft has missed only three parades, two while in the Army.

There have been some changes in the Buzzard format over the century. The mandatory black-face was abandoned in 1958, the Buzzard fife-and-drum corps before that. No longer is the group preceded by a high-poled rack of deer horns, and no longer do they parade back to the Roost after passing the Boston Club.

"But we'll be doing something special for our hundredth march," promises Clarence Lundgren of the city's oldest, grandest and not the most genteel of Carnival marching clubs.

You can make book on it. At 6:30 on Fat Tuesday morning, Buzzards like Kenny Powell, John Scoggins, Butch Acosta and Keith Guise are going to gather where Laurel Street runs into Audubon Park. They'll be talking already about the pit stops ahead, at Norby's, Domilise's, F & M.

Then somebody will hit a bass drum, BOOM-BOOM-BOOM, the march-call for every redblooded New Orleanian, and they will once more come rolling down Laurel and Tchoupitoulas and the rest, and on a hundred blocks the hundred-year-old cry will again be heard: "The Buzzards are coming! Here come the Buzzards!"

Oh, Daddy. It's about time for Mama to get mad again . . .

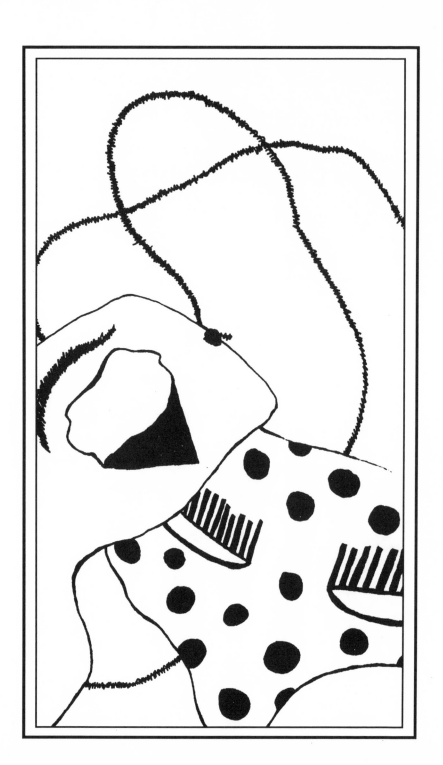

5

Nobody Knows
De Trouble I've Seen

*"Man is born unto trouble,
as the sparks fly upward."*
Book of Job, 5:7

"Count no man happy till you have seen his last day on earth," said the philosopher to the king seeking the secret of happiness. Troubles should be a brake to our envy, seeing that they can come to any one at any time, and that is the best reason to read and write about the suffering of others. . . .

BEING REFEREE IS PART OF JOB

It was just before midnight when patrolmen Michael Conn and Dave Morel get the call that cops hate the most. Code 103 — domestic disturbance.

"We're rolling," Morel said back to the dispatcher. Conn turned the patrol car off St. Claude Avenue and tried not to think about what ugliness might await at the end of the ride. Morel fiddled with his new $100 flashlight. "It's working better," he said. "Must have been cold earlier."

Police buy their own accessories such as guns and flashlights. "Let something look macho, paint it black, and some cop'll buy it," Conn deadpanned.

The call had come from a house on a cracked-sidewalk kind of street, houses slumping toward each other like tired riders on a 5 o'clock bus.

The apartment looked neat. The wife wore jeans and was animated. Her husband had on maroon sweat pants and was surly. Also present were the wife's sister and an older man wearing a fur hat. Everybody was talking at once.

"OK, you'll get your turn," Conn told the husband. "Now you say he slapped you and tried to choke you? Where did this happen?"

The wife's story spilled out fast. She had caught the Claiborne bus in front of Krauss, got off and was walking to pick up her two sons at her sister's when she ran into her ex-husband.

Conn sensed what was coming and asked how the ex-husband, the sons' father, happened to pop up on her sister's street. The wife filibustered, but Conn patiently and persistently pursued an answer.

Hmmph, said the husband, going to sit on the sofa. "This ain't the first time her ex turned up," he said. "So we argued. So I slapped and choked her some."

Conn took a deep breath. He's playing by ear things most of us would say are too important to play by ear. But here, in this troubled room after midnight, there are no judges, no social workers, no marriage counselors. Only a couple of cops wishing they were somewhere else.

"Do you have somewhere you can go tonight and you two can work this out in the daylight?" Conn asked. The wife said yes, her mama's, and moved off to the next room to begin packing things in a grocery bag for herself and her sons.

Bad feelings hovered. Conn walked over to the sofa and softly said to the husband: "You can't get physical, man. You're too big."

"Huh?" grunted the husband, holding his slender arms out for inspection.

"Well, you're too big for her."

Conn turned away and after a while said to the wife, "In the future, you're gonna have to make arrangements for your ex-husband to pick up his kids away from you."

"There ain't no future," the husband snapped from the sofa. "This is over." He got up and headed for the kitchen.

Conn quickly followed him. He's got a buddy, now back on desk duty after three years' recuperation, who didn't follow a husband in a case like this. The man came back with a pistol and put six bullets in the cop's chest.

After a minute, the husband reappeared with a can of Old Milwaukee in his hand. He went up to his wife and took the wedding ring from her finger. Then he took a necklace off her neck. "You ain't gettin' nothing," he said. She went back to packing.

Soon the first of her sons appeared in the front room, a quilt jacket zipped to his chin and a toy ray-gun in his hand. His big eyes stayed on the two uniformed men who had come to take him from his home at midnight and his finger kept pulling the trigger of the ray-gun. Bbrrt. Bbrrt.

Conn asked how old he was, and the boy held up five fingers. "Would you like to ride in a police car?" The boy shook his head hard. "Well, I can't blame you."

The wife was dressing her second son, who had a cast on his leg. Conn asked her where her mother lived and was told an address across town. He grimaced.

Back on the sofa, the husband offered to drive them. "No way, man," Conn told him.

A cab was called and while everyone waited, tension resounded around the clear white walls. The husband sat sullenly. The wife's eyes got wet as she stood hugging the grocery bag. Her sister chatted about something meaningless and the man in the fur hat just shuffled his feet and looked at the floor.

The two boys tried not to look afraid. A cab's horn blew and the wife's sister picked up the boy with a cast on his leg. The wife took the other boy by the hand and moved to the door.

Suddenly her husband got up from the sofa and tried to kiss her on the cheek. She didn't look at him, just headed outside into the dark with the boy at her side pressing that toy trigger. Bbrrt. Bbrrt.

"He's real trigger-happy," Morel joked as he got back in the patrol car. "We'll probably get a call on him someday."

"I wouldn't be at all surprised," Conn said, forgetting to smile.

... As The Romans Did

In the dusk-days of the Roman Empire, the government was feeding 120,000 citizens of Rome and another 80,000 in Constantinople. Some of the upper classes fled to Spain or North Africa, but most just sat around with the lower classes and waited for the end with amazing apathy. There was said to be a real decline in the public spirit . . .

The morning sun hadn't really rolled up its sleeves and gone to work yet, but still there was plenty heat pounding down on the ragged line outside the Incarnate Word school on Apricot Street, and more to come.

Already in the line several umbrellas had been opened against the sun, and there were plenty of wash rags being dabbed against cheeks and necks and bosoms.

Most of the hundred-odd people in the line were old women in summer dresses. Some of them were dragging along two-wheeled shopping carts; many wore terrycloth slippers or shower shoes. All clutched yellow Total Community Action eligibility cards.

On this particular morning, there were lines like this forming at 55 other locations around the city. Inside those locations were brown grocery bags containing free butter, cheese and flour, canned pork and beans, peanut butter, honey and seedless raisins.

For these things, people had begun forming a line here two hours early. They were a line of people-as-pack-animals, the mules and llamas of the Urban Journey, folks with dreams tired and lost, living hard by, right up to, the dollar. They were here to trade another small link, a nick of time, from their moneyless lives for one brown grocery bag with flour and honey inside.

In the middle of the line, an old man mumbled, "You would think they could have a place for people to stand, instead out here in the hot sun."

A nearby old lady answered, "The problem is they don't consider this a poverty area. That's why they only got this one place around here. Now down past Napoleon Avenue . . ."

Another old lady started talking about the glory giveaways of what she called the WPA: "My mama had a big family too, and we got eight quarts of milk a day and eggs loose and fresh."

A middle-aged woman in a flower dress, holding her granddaughter, said, "Don't do no good to be fussing. Like when I go to Charity Hospital, people sitting around cussing. Hey — when I'm there, I'm there. Can leave anytime I want."

A young woman whose T-shirt proclaiming "Life is a Surfing Frenzy" was tightly stretched over her pregnancy, just said, "Lord, I wouldn't be here if I didn't need flour."

At nine, the doors opened. A couple of teenaged boys checked eligibility cards and let in two or three people at a time. First out with her grocery bag was a big woman in a red mumu, her sweaty face showing a sense of loss keenly, very keenly. A young guy with his hair in ringlets peeped in her bag and said, "Some people talk about that cheese, but it's the same thing you buy in the store!" The big woman said she didn't much care for it, but her son liked cheese toast. . . .

A lady in a polka-dot dress said it was her first time, and she was actually waiting in line for a friend who had a doctor's appointment. An old man wearing suspenders said "Uh-huh. Well, that's how you suppose to do, to watch out for each other." The old man had a voice like knives and forks rustling in a silverware drawer.

"Well, I oughta be at the doctor myself," he said, pointing to an infected eye. "Course, I keep me some cold potatoes and grates 'em and puts 'em on and they pulls the fever right outta that eye."

The line moved slowly, time's relativity sharpened by the heat. It was orderly and spoke of the strong sense of connectedness among the poor. Some men waited under a little shade tree on the corner of Cambronne, waited to carry the grocery bags home. A thin old lady carried a leafy switch to control the three small boys tumbling in the little grass between curb and banquette.

"Stop that, you no-good boys!" she hissed as she switched. "Them red bugs gonna get on you and eat you up!"

After a while, a garbage truck coming down Cambronne couldn't pass because of cars parked on both sides of the street. A garbage man with an LSU cap and the saunter of somebody with one short leg got out and began asking whose cars they were.

The corner began to smell bad. A woman with a green T-shirt that read "Newcomb is not negotiable" put down her grocery bag and began fussing.

"Lady, we just trying to get through," the garbage man said. "We might be on our way to pick up your garbage. Nobody picks up your garbage, you get mice."

The woman shut up a moment until the right answer came. "Humph. Well, you ain't doing it for nothing, are you? We pays for you to pick it up. We pays for you to pick it up!" She said it with the jubilance of the righteous taxpayer. Then she picked up her brown grocery bag and waddled away.

That's the way it was going in a land where the dollar is hard to come by, but where esteem and comfort are legal tender for butter and seedless raisins. That's the way it was going this summer morning in the year MCMXC, anno Domini, which is the way the Romans would have written it, only they ain't around anymore . . .

CENTRAL LOCKUP BLUES

You don't want to spend too much time looking around outside Central Lockup.

Just across the street, too close, is Parish Prison's "Tent City," with its rolled wire and olive-drab canvas enclosing ideas and dreams that those outside would rather not know about. At the corners of the yard are the big spotlights with nightmoths seething about like winged wind socks.

Adjacent is an incongruous basketball court surrounded by high razor-topped fences, the city game here to be played by the city's shame. And catty-corner to the court, a bail-bond office with an "open" sign blinking on and off, even on a late Saturday night.

There are signs inside the waitroom of Central Lockup, too. One reads, "No Food or Drink in Lobby Except from Vending Machines. Cheif [sic] Simuel." Except there are no vending machines outside of a couple of cigarette machines. One of them is crippled, the Leaning Tower of cigarette machines.

Another sign reads, "No Loitering. No cameras or picture taking Aollowed [sic]." The signs remind that this is a place of, a place for, shabby humor. A place of, say, 30-by-60, with thick lighting. Two black iron benches on one wall, a bank of four pay phones and one battered section of yellow pages; a few feet from the phones is a half-barred window to an office. In the office is a Christmas tree and some black-shirted criminal sheriff's deputies. From somewhere in the office a radio blares, with much tremolo singing and some clothing store jingles. ("Tell Dailey's who you are and where you work and how you want to pay. For happy, easy credit shopping, try the Dailey's way.")

The office is the buffer between the evening's captives and those who come to try to free them. These are friends and family and fellow sinners, all races, their faces gray and puffy with sleep and worry. If they succeed, if they get a judge to phone or a bondsman to relent, they can get the sinner out in three or four molasses hours.

One of the first to be released on this evening is a woman taken in on a DWI. Her husband has been waiting, in a dirty gray T-shirt, his eyes avoiding human contact and scanning the walls for a clock that's not there. When the bars of the holding cell clang open, she comes out and says something soft to him. He is trying for disgust, but can only manage disappointment. They move to the door. He walks urgently, with his right shoulder held low, like a man being pulled by a large dog.

Five Vietnamese men, all young, come in. They are lucky enough that one of the deputies is Vietnamese, too. He comes to the half-barred window and talks to them in the native tongue for a long time. They listen, motionless, all with their hands folded behind their backs. Then they move to a corner of the room to parley, two of the men hunkering down on their heels in the old country fashion. Then they leave, something ventured, nothing gained.

The same thing will happen to a middle-aged, deaf mute couple who try to communicate with a deputy by means of a young sign language translator. The last thing he translates is, "It is very frustrating to try to say what we want to say like this."

It will go on like this 'til late morning, every morning. In a week, scores of bonded offenders will shuffle through this room, dazed and featureless, at least momentarily beyond redemption. Some will never see another booking officer again in their lives. Some will see more of booking officers than they ever saw of their fathers.

In the wee hours of the morning, three young men, Cracker-accented and still drunk, come rumbling in. They are Florida boys who'd been to the Van Halen concert in Biloxi the night before and came here "because we'd never been to Bourbon Street before." One of their group, Jamie, had done something to a sign saying, "Support our Troops," and some cops put the snatch on him. They found a pocketknife. The bail is $500 for the concealed weapon and $300 for public drunkenness, but since they're from out of town, they couldn't get a bondsman to cooperate.

One of the three, Jerry, says he is the son of a Pensacola judge and wants to argue with the deputy that the knife in question had a blade less than four inches long. "No matter if it's two inches long, long as it's concealed," says the deputy. "Now if your daddy's really a judge, have him call this number and we'll tell him what to do."

When he talks to a deputy, Jerry is patronizingly polite. But away from the window, he snarls. "If I get my old man on the phone, he'll have somebody's ass!" Problem is, Jerry's old man won't answer the phone. "Damn it, I know he's home. It's 3:30 in the morning there."

Drunkest of the Pensacola group is Anthony. While Jerry spars with long-distance operators, Anthony keeps lurching back to the window, asking for a match and a latrine in a drunk-deep voice. Officer Murray comes to the window and it's lucky she's good-humored. "You take it easy, son," she tells him.

After an hour or two, the Florida boys give up and head back to the motel, leaving Jamie to think about how safe and secure is Pensacola.

Twenty minutes later, the holding cell opens and out comes Kim in a dark windbreaker and faded jeans. She's a little darker than the color of cornflakes, hair some stringy shade of orange, and somewhere between a girl and a woman. She seems at first to have a benevolence about herself and all the deputies seem to know her.

"What happened to your hair?" Officer Murray asks. "I know you wasn't born with that color." And everyone laughs.

Kim's friend David is still locked up. "It was his birthday," she says. "We was just on the corner 'n' shit. Clowning 'n' shit." The deputy says there's an attachment out on David and bail is going to be $3,200.

The deputy goes off. The radio is playing an over-dramatic, falsetto version of "Silent Night." The girl-woman named Kim turns her head to stare at the crippled cigarette machine. She's not smiling anymore. Now she's just another Saturday night someone waiting at Central Lockup for her man.

THE ANGOLA EXPRESS

The names have been changed to protect the innocent. The guilty, too.

It's the bus trip nobody really likes to take and the fare just went up.

"Sorry, folks," says the big pipe-puffing man in the red jacket, representing Baptiste Bus Lines. "But we just don't have enough riders this morning to pay for the driver and insurance. So we're gonna have to ask for twenty dollars instead of fifteen."

A low murmur ripples through the bus' eight passengers. Then Lovey, an older woman in flowered dress and rings on every finger of her left hand, holds up a twenty and shouts, "OK, OK! Come get the money and let's get on the road! I gotta go!"

All the riders have to go, go whenever they can. Leave their linoleumed roomettes and their project sofas and get to the corner of South Claiborne and Jackson before 8 a.m. Get aboard the unmarked three-axle bus called "The Angola Express," for a three-hour ride to the state's largest penitentiary.

It's a hard destination and getting there is hard. The bus wings off the interstate past Vicari Hall in Kenner, then back on, pushing hard, up to jouncing speed, into LaPlace and a short stop at McDonald's. Brenda is a large young woman with a two-year-old son sucking on a green ninny bottle. She wasn't expecting the fare-bump to twenty, so she's short. Lovey buys the baby some snacks. "We all together," Lovey tells Brenda.

On the road again, highway jolts sling Mickey Dee's thin coffee around. Willie Mae tries to sleep under a white bath towel, then gives it up. Dot, a big woman wearing a church T-shirt that proclaims, "Christ is the answer. I love you and there's nothing you can do about it," doesn't even try to sleep. The bus radio wails earnestly about Love and Baby and Girl and Promises and keeps people awake. Besides, by the time the ride turns onto Highway 66, joints are getting stiff, stiff as the joints of a body that has carried a son now old enough to be in jail can get.

So in the back of the bus, Dot and Lovey and Willie Mae talk about the cost of crime. Not the $20,296 it costs the taxpayer to lock a man up for a year; this is the cost to the convict's family, money and mind.

"I send my son $40 a week," says Willie Mae. "My first phone bill was for $300. But how can you not accept when they call?"

"Yeah, baby," agrees Dot. "At first, it haunted my heart. People thought I'd lost my mind. But I keep believing God is working on something and one day those gates are gonna open."

As the bus pulls up to those gates, Lovey takes out a bottle of perfume and shares a dab with Dot.

While the women and children are being processed and frisked at the Main Gate, a call goes out for their men. They begin to come in, from the vegetable sheds, the cotton fields, and the mattress factory. Past the rows of men swinging scythes and being watched by guards on horseback. Past the K-9 dog kennel and its marked graves. Past the inmate cemetery and its unmarked graves.

They are men whose perturbed hearts or wanton destinies have separated them from those who care. They write letters to the prison newspaper that say ". . . jury didn't physically put my wife behind bars. But if you love the man enough to want to stand by his side no matter what, then you too are imprisoned as long as he is."

The Visitor's Hall is where the imprisoned meet those who want to stand by their side, no matter what.

"We've got 5,200 inmates here, but only a small percentage get any visitors," says Lt. Mary Smith, who runs the Main Prison's Visitor's Hall. When she was a girl, Smith picked cotton in Franklin Parish, so she knows about people and hard times. She doesn't have much trouble with inmates here.

"Even two mortal enemies that can't live together, in here they can sit at the next table and make no fuss. They don't wanta lose this privilege."

The rules are simple. No table-hopping, no excessive displays of affection. If someone needs talking to, Smith calls him away from the table. "If you blow on someone in front of his family, even the meekest man's gonna blow back."

Almost every inmate, meek or mean, tells his family he was "set up," he is innocent. Almost every family believes it or wants to. There's the story of the old prison guard who snickered like most guards at all the "innocent" stories. Then his own grandson came to Angola, and the old man had no trouble at all believing the boy was innocent.

Can the heart pardon as fast as the eye can see, as fast as the memory can deposit? Yes it can, yes it can.

Just watch the visitors laugh with the visited, share Camel cigarettes and homemade ice cream, be brave when the jailhouse tales of suicide and failed parole hearings are told.

Dot's son Tim talks about his pal Herb, who got bit on the ear in a fight and is sweating out an HIV test. Willie Mae's son Mike says, "This place is The Twilight Zone. But if I can work here for 18 cents an hour, I can work outside for $5 an hour." Brenda's husband Ron says, "Guys in here for a long time wanna get their head a certain way to deal with this place, so they cut themselves off from everyone. But I need her."

Three o'clock. Last Polaroids, last hugs and kisses are exchanged. The visitors file out to an old Bluebird bus for the ride back to the Main Gate. Inside, they feel the loss all over again.

"I usta leave here saying 'Lawd almighty! Look where they done put my child!'" says Willie Mae.

"I'm glad Timmy's working in the kitchen now," says Dot. "In the fields, they lose too much weight."

The Bluebird jogs past two dusty rows of convicts moving down the road with hoes over their shoulders. Hard, profane men. They see the bus, recognize its cargo, the women who are here with them somehow, the women who remember well the well-forgotten.

As the bus rambles on toward freedom's gate, the men raise their hoes in silent salute.

THE REAL ER

'And if there be an opportunity of serving one who is a stranger in financial straits, give full assistance to all such. For where there is love of man, there is also love of the art."

Hippocrates, *Father of Medicine*, circa 410 B.C.

— Can you get a sense of what goes on here on a single Friday night? Or does it take 50 Fridays, or 500?

Dr. Keith Van Meter has spent many Fridays in this ant farm of medical need and response. He is 50 years old and works a hundred hours a week. He is intelligence with a plebeian face and has the energy that keeps toes pushing against shoe-tops. Still, for a man with so much to say, he knows how to listen.

Just now he is listening to the offshore worker, whose brown boots sprawl in front of the bed. The worker's body is a shield covered with tattooist heraldry and he is showing the doctor where it hurts. From here (a bluebird tattoo) to here (a unicorn). The pain has knocked his whiskeypride out and he's admitting he smokes and drinks too much, way too much.

"I think I need some morphine," he says. "'Cuz I'm hurtin' real bad. From here to here. I ain't kiddin'."

Van Meter moves on, checking the 30-odd beds in the room. He is trailed by an entourage of young residents and nurses, everyone slightly harried but staying cool. After they move away from the bedside of a guy who's drunk insecticide, one murmurs, "Betcha his X-rays won't show any bugs."

Though he constantly cautions the young residents about their M.A.S.H.-like gallows humor, Van Meter understands the self-preserving need of it.

"You go through several stages of cynicism about patients," he says a little later. "You can never lose your authority, like with kids. But hopefully, after all the stages, you'll come back to forgiveness."

"Charity's like a sanctuary for this city, a medical cathedral. It's the last place where most of these people are going to get the benefit of the doubt. The tattooed fella? You might think he's just trying to get morphine, but I think he may have an infark. If you get socially judgmental, you're fried."

— "You come to love these people," says a registered nurse, Faith. "I come from a small town in Alabama, and you'd never see anything like this there. Sometimes they say 'blood clogs' for 'blood clots' and 'peanut-butterball' for 'phenobarbital,' but they're good people and that's why you work at Charity. Even if it means you're responsible for twice as many patients as at a private hospital."

Faith doesn't have a last name on her nametag and she wears her ID backwards. Why? "Oh, lots of us do that." she says, smiling. "You know how it is. We get some people who swear they're gonna come back here and kill us."

— There is no time for names here. The staff refers to the patients by their condition or symptoms. But it is a place where pain wears dirty pants, panic a flowered dress . . .

In a bed by the wall, a wiry man in oily gaberdine pants begins to thrash and howl. One resident grabs his wrists and bends one over the guardrail. Another pins his ankles, and a pretty nurse stumbles away and calls for security. She tries hard to stay calm, begins scribbling a report in triplicate and mutters, "He tried to bite me." The resident holding the guy's wrists says, "I think we have a petit mal seizure. He told me he could smell it coming." The one holding the guy's ankles says, "We were about to sign him out. Ten more minutes, he'd been gone."

— In the hallway by the nurse's station, a woman in a flowered dress sits in a wheelchair. Her eyes are bloodshot and her wrists are fastened to the wheelchair by leather handcuffs. She alternately shrieks and gospelmoans to be set free. An older lady passes by and the woman in the wheelchair hails her: "Couldja get me a cold drink?" The older woman waits while the wheelchair woman shakes fifty cents from a coin purse in her lap. As she moves off in search of the soft drink, the woman in the flowered dress calls piteously after her: "You gonna come back, huh? You ain't gonna take my money?"

Then she begins shrieking that she wants to go home. A passing nurse winks at a friend and whispers, "Another satisfied customer."

— In the waiting room of Fast-Track, lowest priority of the ER, sit two prisoners wearing OPP denim shirts. Both are handcuffed and each is watched by a uniformed guard from Parish Prison. A passing nurse eyes them and when she is out of earshot, dryly notes, "We have a saying around here: The life you save may end up taking yours."

— Patrick Reed, RN, knows about the self-healing power of humor, knows how many of the staff will go to Joe's Lounge on Cleveland or the St. Charles Tavern after the shift is over to talk of the guy in gaberdine or the woman in the flowered dress. Looking for laughter, that last-ditch stand against fear and fatigue.

"The altruistic desire to help people is part of it, but people are mainly here for the experience," Reed says. "That's why we have a high turnover, people get experience and other hospitals want 'em. That and the fact that the heat here never goes down. You never know what's coming through that door — and it's almost always something bad."

Reed can't chat anymore. Through the door has just come a backyard mechanic. A Toyota transmission has fallen on his chest.

— Sometime later, Van Meter checks on the tattoo man. There are a couple of tubes and wires attached to him, but he sleeps the untroubled sleep of a baby, the unicorn rising and falling rhythmically.

"You know why he's sleeping? Liquid nitroglycerine. See, he was having heart trouble. As a young doctor, I'da been certain he was faking, just drug-seeking."

Dr. Keith Van Meter, healer in a hurry, pauses to smile. He's not such a young doctor anymore, and he's come to a place of forgiveness. He looks very much like he likes it there, too.

AFTER THE FALL

On the corner just outside the Winn-Dixie parking lot, Joe had fallen and couldn't get up.

It was good that the hot sun was sponging up the morning rain from the sidewalk and it was not too damp where Joe was half-sitting, half-laying.

He was not alone. A tall, husky cop was already on the scene and so were two EMT types, a young man and woman, talking on their radios to someone back at headquarters. There was also a stream of supermarket shoppers coming in and out of the parking lot. Most passing cars slowed down for a look, and their braking tires hissed against the wet street.

"No, no mister!" the cop said. Joe was trying to get up, grabbing for the bus-stop obelisk that tilted drunkenly to the ground. The EMT woman tucked her radio into its holster and went over to the fallen guy. She squatted down next to him and put a gentle hand on his cheek. "Stay down please, sir. We're going to take care of you, but you've got to stay down," she said.

It was hard to gauge how much Joe understood of what he was hearing. He tilted his head back to the pavement, blinked and took some deep breaths. Then he tried again to get up.

The EMT woman looked around for some help. The cop sighed and sauntered over. He looked to be the kind who joined the force because of the uniform: skin-tight pants, cleaner-crisp shirt, gleaming black shoes. And he moved to his duty as if he didn't want to get the uniform messy, even though there was no blood or spittle or indeed any of life's shameful liquids around.

It wasn't likely that Joe was going to do much to mess up anybody's uniform. He looked near 70 and the dusty bones of age weren't being much help to him now. When the cop put a hand on his shoulder, he lay back down with his eyes open and looked up at the blue sky.

A passing shopper stopped to question the cop, who had straightened up and backed away from his task, smoothing his trousers as he went. "Did he get hit by the bus?" the shopper asked.

She was young and close to pretty, close enough to interest the cop. "He's probably in a state of intoxication," the cop said with the Latinate formality of the paramilitary.

Joe had the pathetic air of a cloth doll, but not one dressed in a drunkard's clothes. He was wearing a light plaid shirt, clean slacks and slightly frayed Hush Puppies, and through everything he kept his navy blue hat on. The hat, probably a Homberg, was not in keeping with summer heat.

He looked like the kind of guy who had grown kids out there somewhere, maybe even a respectable personnel record on file with some company. But the touch of gold had apparently long since hurried on to bless other lives and leave his alone. . . .

At the moment his stasis was almost total. The two EMT workers knelt next to him and talked to him in low voices. A snaggle-toothed man came from somewhere and began talking to the cop. He must have known the man on the ground and was telling what he knew. There was grease in his hair and on his shirt, and he looked like whiskey had not served him well. From time to time, he would look down and say, "Joe . . . Joe! Just stay still, Joe. These people are gonna help you. Just stay still."

After a while, the guy from EMT looked up grinning and said, "He says he's from Africa," and he jerked a thumb in the direction of Joe's color of fresh-washed Venetian blinds. The cop rolled his eyes.

An ambulance pulled up and a man and woman got out. The EMT guy straightened up and walked over. "He's drunk. He fell down three times," the EMT guy said to the ambulance driver. Both seemed to find this on the funny side.

The ambulance team unloaded a wheeled gurney and what looked like a yellow surfboard. You could catch sight of Joe's eyes, which would widen and flutter from time to time. The eyes were by turn dreamy and desperate and made you wonder what remarkable images and impressions they were corralling from the unremarkable surroundings.

The ambulance driver reached for the Homberg, and panic came to Joe's eyes. He began to thrash around and grabbed his hat by the brim. "Easy, easy!" pleaded Snaggletooth. "He gets like that about his hat. He loves his hat. He never takes it off."

The EMT guy went around behind Joe's head and grabbed both his wrists lightly and pulled his arms back behind his head. "He'll take it off now," muttered the ambulance driver and plucked off the Homberg. Then he rolled Joe onto the yellow surfboard. One of the medical people locked a neckbrace onto Joe while another sliced strips of adhesive tape. Then they began taping Joe to the surfboard in five places: forehead, neck, belly, thighs and ankles. He got very red in the face.

Snaggletooth picked up the Homberg and laid it on Joe's chest. Someone asked the cop to help lift the surfboard onto the gurney. The cop made a face. "I hope I don't hurt my back on this," he grunted.

Somebody produced Joe's two-toned umbrella and offered it to Snaggletooth. But Joe's pal now yielded to the tyranny of time. Either he was embarrassed to have taken up the time of so many professional people or had remembered he had somewhere to go. Now he seemed in a hurry to quit the scene. He waved the umbrella away and the driver tucked it alongside Joe on the gurney. Some hospital pilferer would be glad.

The only dignity of the final demarcation was in sight-gag humor. The useless umbrella, the mummifying adhesive tape, the belly-balanced Homberg . . .

"I'm going out to Kenner," grunted the cop. "Get me a nice easy job."

Nearby, an ample woman, carrying the wisdom of the past, bore a big umbrella against the sun. She sipped at a 20-oz. diet drink.

Snaggletooth paused in front of her and said, "There ain't no nice way to get old."

The woman sipped and chortled: "That's right, baby! You said something there!"

6

When You're Smiling

*"Better by far you should
forget and smile than that you
should remember and be sad."*
Christina Rossetti
Remember

The title of another song great in marching parades. It's hard but gratifying work to get people to smile. When I started writing for newspapers, an old-timer told me that if you set out to make your audience cry but couldn't pull it off, nothing was lost and they'd forgive you. But if you set out to make them laugh and didn't succeed . . .

ARMADILLOS AND THE MAN

There had been spoor: deep gougings on the ground which I, full of shirk, had tried to pass off as major construction of moon-crazed crawfish. She was having none of it.

"Crawfish never build like that," she insisted.

"Well, if you're comfortable with the word *never*," I sniffed. "Myself, I'm not an expert on crustacean behavior."

She would not be moved, this lovely lady, this little Light of Mine (LOM). Some pesky visitor had informed her that her wonderful yard in a rustic section of Covington was being torn up by armadillos. Delay in removing the varmints could only result in the collapse of her house and soil erosion.

"Can you do anything at all to help?" she mildly demanded. My first two impulses were to swiftly answer, "No." The third was: here is a fleeting, fading chance to provide the protection that history had demanded of men until about 1964. "I'll go down to the feed store and see what I can learn about armadillos," I mumbled bravely.

At the feed store off Columbia Street, I discovered the following: (1) The armadillos were looking for grubs, (2) scattering lime on the ground burns their feet and makes them leave, (3) they carry the AIDS virus in their blood, and (4) the cost of the humane Havahart traps is only slightly less than a down payment on a Lexus.

It was that last fact that spurred a feeling of shame. Would Kit Carson, Jim Bridger or Jeremiah Johnson choose such wimpy solutions? "I'll be back next weekend," I growled to LOM. "Loaded for armadillo."

On the drive over the Causeway the next Friday, I thought about my adversary. I had never realized that they got into people's yards. From the number of armadillo omelets I'd seen on highways, I'd just assumed they never made it across any roads. Now it was them or me, on the killing grounds of Covington.

LOM was full of little anxieties as I made ready. "You can't shoot him with that rifle. I've got neighbors all around." "It's a pellet gun. The rifle's still in the car." "What's with the satsumas and rhubarbs?" "Well, I gotta bait the area and I didn't know where to buy grubs. Those things were on sale."

She also seemed to poke fun at my hunter's-orange vest, my Walkman and my flask filled with Christian Brothers Frost White Brandy. "I tried hunting sober once," I testily replied. "It made the gnats much harder to bear and made the other hunters mad at me."

"*I'm* not a hunter," she said coyly. "I'm a hunter-gatherer. I gather hunters. I'm sure you're going to get him" LOM is such an optimist that she always believes she's going to win the lottery, even though she never buys a ticket.

Secretly, I figured I had a better chance of hauling a rainbow trout out of the London Avenue canal, but I went to the yard to cut a dashing figure. I laid out the rhubarbs and satsumas, set up my folding chair, pumped up the Daisy Model 856, set my Dorcy 6-volt floating lantern alongside . . .

I surveyed the sprawling yard. On three sides, a retired sheriff, a hag and a yard full of Welsh Corgis who howl at the flight of a bumble-bee. On the east was a creek and beyond that, a hundred yards of woods. In my field of fire were only an azalea bush, an iron-plated kettle and, presiding over a peony arrangement, a statue of Francis of Assisi, well-known saint and animal lover.

From the Walkman came Slim Whitman: *I'm brown as a berry . . . from ridin' the prairie.* A west wind sidled up to the yard-leaves. I drowsed.

I awakened to a moon-splashed specter, a nine-banded Dasypus armadillo, moving north to south. The creature looked like Roseanne would if she had four legs — the facial resemblances were quite remarkable — and hurried toward a ducal-sized table of hon-eyed ham and Baby Swiss.

I flipped on the lantern and the creature froze, red-eyed. With a jerky movement, I raised the Daisy and squeezed off a shot and, near as I could tell, popped the monster right in the carapace. He whirled half-round to face me, then followed a series of noises, in this sequence: (1) a basso-profundo hiss from him, on the order of an aroused Tyrannosaurus Rex, (2) a Mezzo-soprano shriek from me as I tumbled from the chair to my posterior rugae, and (3) an alto howl from the Welsh Corgis across the street.

On the way inside, my internal voice cried, "Lemme getcha on a highway — I got a Chrysler'll make mincemeat outtaya." But the accent was that of the cowardly lion in *Wizard of Oz.*

LOM was worried. "What happened? I heard you squeal." "I was yelling at the dogs," I grunted. "They scared him off before I could get a shot."

The next evening, I started early. Painting white-out on the sights of my Marlin .22 rifle. Crimping the bulletheads of the mini-mags for a more shattering impact. "You look so serious it gives me the creeps," said LOM. "It's the archetype of males preparing for the hunt," I said grimly. "The mastodon trembles when that happens."

She wished me a pleasant stalk, but that was like saying good-night to an insomniac. I settled down, switched some Marty Robbins gunfighter ballads on the Walkman to wire up my mood. *Here to do some business . . . with the Big Iron on his hip.*

I saw him early, sticking his snout into the ground and twisting his body around to make a conical hole. As I pushed the rifle's safety off with my thumb, he started to amble away in a weird gait, back heels, front claws.

Just as my finger brought my trigger back to me, the armadillo jumped straight up like they sometimes do under your car as they run across the highway. The bullet went under him, hit the kettle, then ricocheted to shear away two fingers off St. Francis of Peonies, which is the way he probably preferred things. The Corgis were spectacularly quiet.

LOM ran out, surveyed the scene, cupped her hand behind her ear. "Ah, I'm listening for the trembling of the mastodons," she murmured wickedly.

"Lime," I muttered. "I'm gonna check out that lime."

HADACOL EASY TO SWALLOW

Until the Hadacol Kid came along, the only elixir I knew of was Dr. Tichenor's.

Pinky Vidacovich would come on the radio and sing: "*Now Gabied's throat was always sore / he always wore a frown / since he gargled him with Tichenor's / his voice you cannot drown / That good old Dr. Tichenor's / best antiseptic in town.*"

About the same time, a new boy came to the neighborhood, one we dubbed the Hadacol Kid. He always wore a T-shirt emblazoned with the new tonic's official mascot, a Supermanlike creature named Captain Hadacol.

"It's a magic tonic my maw makes me drink," the Hadacol Kid bragged. "It'll make you stronger'n Tarzan and Red Ryder." He proceeded to whip us all arm-rasslin' and demonstrate that henceforth he would be the law south of Canal Street.

We all ran home immediately and placed our orders for Hadacol with our parents. "It's fulla alcohol, something for winos," my father sniffed.

Everyone in Louisiana had an opinion on Hadacol in 1950. The first batch had been cooked up in a wooden barrel in a Delcambre barn about five years earlier. It tasted foul, but quaffers said it made them feel sassy as a young rooster.

The idea was seized upon by state Sen. Dudley J. LeBlanc, or Coozan Dud, as he was known to his many Cajun friends. Someone in my family swore that Coozan Dud had once been discovered recycling coffins to increase the profits of his burial insurance business in south Louisiana, but I don't know if that's so. He certainly proved to be a master at promoting Hadacol.

During its brief life, Hadacol became the best-selling patent medicine in American history. A tune called "Hadacol Boogie" blared from every radio. There were Captain Hadacol comic books and a Hadacol Caravan, a traveling show with stars such as Bob Hope and Hank Williams.

But greatest of the tonic's promotions were the testimonial ads. Real people claimed relief from anemia, neuritis, asthma, high and low blood pressure, TB and "stomach distress."

One of the most astounding claims was from a Kentucky woman who wrote to the *Louisville Courier-Journal* that she had mistakenly added Hadacol instead of vanilla to her angel cake. She wound up tossing the batter to the chickens. "Well, sir, since eating that Hadacol batter, my old rooster crows continually," the woman wrote. "And my hens are laying bigger and better eggs, day by day. At this writing, my eggs are so big I am realizing 45 cents a dozen, in contrast to the market price of 24 cents a dozen."

Truth is, some modern nutritionists claim that Coozan Dud's brew was not bad for its time. It had a lot of minerals and vitamins, particularly in the B series, that were missing from the meat-and-potato diets of the 1940s. It also contained niacin, iron, honey and 12 percent alcohol.

There were plenty jokes about the alcohol, but Coozan Dud didn't mind. Once, on a radio show, Groucho Marx asked him what his product was good for.

"Last year it was good for five-and-a-half million dollars for me," LeBlanc replied.

Hadacol faded as fast as it had come. Coozan Dud ran unsuccessfully for governor and died unwealthy in 1971.

The Hadacol mystique died even quicker in my neighborhood. The Hadacol Kid got in an argument with Johnny and Mike from Bienville Street. Their granny was widely held — even by adults — to be a hoodoo lady, so they feared no magic elixir alive, not even one with B vitamins. Johnny threw a punch, Mike threw another, and there was the Hadacol Kid, flat on his back and crying like somebody's sister.

We all ran home immediately and canceled our Hadacol orders. No sense tasting something that bad if you were going to end up flat on your back anyhow.

FALLEN GAMBLERS

Something was wrong with the timing and function of the thing, like seeing a car riding in sunshine with its headlights on . . .

Three straight times I had split pairs and bumped up my bet and three straight times the dealer — a lady with plenty hair and no smile — had dealt herself twenty-one. The last time had taken five cards, and as each one flipped over, I felt like I'd swallowed another bit of octopus cooked in its own ink.

"Not my day," I croaked bravely. "I'll come back later." The dealer nodded politely, but doubt was correctly written all over her mascara.

I groped my way to the door, images of impatient creditors flashing before my eyes. It was suddenly equator-hot; had the Harrah's management shut off the air conditioning because of lower-than-expected revenues? I had certainly done my part to boost the take. . . .

Maybe it was the tardy arterial flow that hatched my next idea; perhaps it was only congenital stupidity. Anyhow, I stopped at the change booth and got my last fiver turned into quarters. I put the quarters into a plastic cup and stepped outside to look around.

On the bottom step half-sat, half-sprawled a young woman in an indigo-colored sheath dress. She wasn't looking at me, so I figured this was as good a time as any.

I hooked the railing under my armpit to make the fall as gentle as possible. Then I carefully turned over the cupful of quarters, shouted, "You diaper rash!" or some other malediction, and half-sat, half-sprawled on the third step.

I began to make the grimaces of a man who's just been bitten by a Komodo dragon. The Indigo Gal looked unimpressed.

"Hey, sucker!" she growled softly. "You trying some kinda slip-and-fall mess? Well, I'm already here!"

I looked around carefully and saw no one else. "Well, I thought you was just waitin' for a cab," I growled back. "Besides, I can't very well get up and do it again somewhere else, can I?"

Indigo Gal just shrugged. "There ain't been nobody around to

103

check on me yet," she said.

We sprawled together for a couple of minutes. It was starting to look like this was gonna take some time, so I asked what she did.

"I'm a welfare mother. What do you do?"

I thought for a minute. "I'm the male equivalent of a welfare mother."

After a time, a young Japanese couple strolled by. He stopped to take some pictures of us, then he motioned for me to take a snapshot of him and his wife.

"I can't get up," I tried to explain. "I've invested plenty money here and now time, too. Maybe you two could go stand by the Louie Armstrong statue, and I'll take it sitting here. At that distance, you'll probably look like crab lice, but the folks back in Kyoto will recognize Louie."

As they walked over to Louie's statue, Indigo Gal whispered, "Is that a Nikon? You oughta shag on outta here with it."

A little while later, a guy in platform shoes came by, walking his Bichon frise. "I hope you two realize there's hidden cameras aimed at the steps," he tittered. "So let's hope you both took a real showbiz fall!"

"Thanks for your gift of humor," I shouted after him, having no fear of a Bichon frise whatsoever. "Yeah, funny," added Indigo Gal. "Funny like a three-dollar bill."

Our next visitor was a 12-year-old skateboarder eating salted peanuts. He squatted next to some of my spilled quarters. "If you ever wanted to play guitar or catch touchdown passes, you're gonna need all your fingers," I warned, and he understood promptly.

"Sure is hot out here," said Indigo Gal. "This really might work, if you wanta know the truth."

"Look," I told the skateboarder, "pick up some of my change here and go get me and the lady here some snowballs and get yourself one, too. I'll take Spearmint. Just leave your skateboard here for collateral."

The boy wanted to know how come we wouldn't scram with his skateboard.

"Fool!" said Indigo Gal. "I got an investment here! You think

I'm gonna lose it over some skateboard? Make mine Bubble Gum."

Fifteen minutes later, he was back. With two snowballs only. He handed one to Indigo Gal and licked fiercely at the other. "I dropped yours," he explained, blithely.

I was just about to see how far I could throw a skateboard from a sitting position when a security cop walked up. Indigo Gal's legs began to struggle beneath her. "Don't you see me trying to get up?" she demanded. "I can't see you getting up because I never saw you fall," the cop said, calmly. He looked me over. "You must be new at this. We got cameras just for this sorta thing."

Indigo Gal stopped trying to get up and got sassy instead. "That Committee for 25,000 New Jobs — where's dem jobs? The casino was supposed to put money in the co-mu-nit-tee and that's what I'm trying to do here. If you don't put money in the community, how's the community gonna afford the casino?"

Just then a callow casino employee came out with a cardboard sign and began taping it to the wall. The sign read: "Watch out for fallen gamblers." He looked at us kindly and said, "Been here long? The man in charge of fallen customers left at two for his grandson's graduation from summer camp. Come back tomorrow, OK?"

Indigo Gal got up and slowly dusted the back of her sheath dress. "Tomorrow, I'll take the St. Ann Street side and you take the St. Peter. It looks bad when we bunch up like this."

RONNIE'S RESUME

Hon. Edwin W. Edwards
Governor's Mansion

Dear Excellency,

It has come to my attention that there remain problems with your appointments to the state Casino Board. I think I can help, and I hereby offer my services to that board. Here's why I would be a highly suitable selection:

• Not only am I a political animal, but all of my family members have been Mid-City Democrats since the days of Grover Cleveland. I myself drove a sound truck throughout Lakeview on the night before the general election in 1972, broadcasting "Vote for Treen" at maximum volume. Once at a family reunion, my Uncle Philly quoted from H.L. Mencken that picking a politician was like buying bootleg liquor: "You never know what you're getting, but you know it isn't what it says it is." Uncle Philly was never invited to another reunion and was denied burial in the family plot.

• In your last campaign versus David Duke, I submitted a bumper sticker slogan to your election committee ("Edwards: A Grifter for All the People") but it lost out to "Vote for the Crook. It's Important." I see now that my slogan wasn't impudent enough.

• I know you are a very spiritual man, one who practices several religions simultaneously. I would like you to know that I read the Bible daily. Looking for loopholes.

• You could not be accused of lowering the collective intelligence of the Casino Board by appointing me. I have authored two books ("Suicide for Optimists" and "White Flight: The Next Generation") and have read several others.

• Since this appointment concerns the regulation of gambling, I would like to present my gambling credentials: (1) For several years I was a regular at the Friday night dice games at Fats 'n' Russ'. While it is true that such games were illegal throughout the state at that time, we were exempt by a "local option" covering the registered voters of the area bounded by Tulane, Gravier, S. Clark and

S. Genois streets. (2) My family never saw a domesticated animal they didn't bet on. Uncle Bob once took a broken-down thorough-bred to Arabi, where it could be advertised and sold as an "Arabian."

• I hope that my familiarity with gambling will not automatically disqualify me from service on the Casino Board.

• Like Gilbert Lainez, I am Sherman Copelin's brother-in-law and, like Gilbert, I was a juror at one of your trials. I forget exactly which one, but I clearly recall getting plenty of laughs from my fellow jurors by drawing a Charlie Chaplin mustache on a photograph of prosecutor John Volz. It was the type of witticism that would have appealed to your raffish sense of humor, and I like to think it played some small part in the mistrial. As you said about Gilbert, it would be "poetic justice" for me to now get a gubernatorial appointment.

• I want to assure you of my sympathy for the likes of Mr. Gus Mijalis and his family of consultants to the gaming industry. I would certainly be mindful of the difficulty involved in having a family leader in jail, unless, of course, the family name is Roemer. What gaming opponents like Mr. Forgotston term "nepotism," I see as a sharing of family values — a virtue cynically confiscated by Republicans in recent elections.

• To illustrate the level of creative imagination I would bring to the Casino Board, permit me to offer this proposal: After reading the interview of your wife, Candy, I was taken by her statement that she gambled "and I'm good at it . . . I can't throw fours, but I'm good at sixes and eights." I propose that Candy become the chief spokeswoman for the Louisiana gaming industry, demonstrating how easy it is to win at craps. And surely her fees could help cushion your retirement. . . .

• I know the principles of the practice of what is called "Check-kiting." This knowledge derives from my former employment as a bank-runner for "Bogus" Bob Daspit's Exxon station and would enable me to evaluate the FBI's notoriously judgmental report on Jazzville's Burnell Moliere in a fair and impartial manner.

• It is a harsh but inescapable fact that any of your appointments will be closely scrutinized by the news media. I know these people, and how they turn their heads with reckless abandon when the waiter approaches with the check. I have the names and dates of those who never miss a hospitality suite. I know one who has a stolen receipt pad from Holiday Inn, but actually always stays at Motel 3s, the half-price versions of Motel 6s. I know which one does his most creative writing on his expense accounts. Armed with this knowledge, I am in no way daunted by possible assaults from these social parasites.

• By all accounts you have ceased your attentions to what one news reporter uncharitably described as *bimbo du jour*. But should you ever change your mind, I have a cousin who is as fine as frog's hair and was only heard to say No one time — and that was because she misunderstood the question.

• Rumor has it that receiving an appointment from you involves the appointee eating grass on his knees while saying over and over, "I am your cow." I hope this is no longer necessary, but I would like it known that I prefer a nice rye grass with a good vinaigrette.

• In summary, I am not a man of many wishes. Though my finances are crowding zero, I am one of the world's great deficit spenders. I use the truth sparingly, but have never been caught in a major lie. Thus, I believe I could truthfully be described as "a typical Edwards appointee."

• Forgive the length of this missive, but it is caused by my excitement of being proximate to your fabled generosity.

Worshipfully,
Ronnie Virgets
Citizen and Frequent Voter

MOVING VIOLATIONS

Surely, I am thinking, *personal happiness* is based on some balance. The man said simplify. Such things as worldliness and greediness must not play too big a role. . . .

These thoughts come to me as I find myself up to my very damp armpits in half-unpacked U-Haul boxes. It must have been some imbalance of worldliness and greediness that drove me to abandon my four crowded downtown rooms for these seven rooms, plus basement, in Uptown.

That's Uptown with a capital "U." Tennis clubs, people with sunglasses pushed to the tops of their heads, Carnival balls. Krewe of Antediluvians. Mystik Knights of Affluence. Maybe I could become part of it. Maybe me and my gal could make one of those alliterative society columns: "That fun duo frolicked through another fashionable Friday fete."

Yeah, well now I'm here and I'm ready to call the ACLU and talk about cruel and unusual punishment.

It all began on moving day. Fortunately the Mistress of the Manor has some grown kids who have friends and they did all the heavy lifting. I kept walking up and down stairs carrying sewing baskets and tins of animal crackers. My chest was heaving so that on certain inhalations it actually exceeded the size of my waist. Then I got a phone call from a conspicuously absent pal.

"So how's moving?" he chirped. "I moved in 1974, and I said then my next move was to the Garden of Memories and then I'd be traveling light. Ha-ha."

"Come by and see us," I wheezed. "But wait for the written invitation."

The landlord showed up without an invitation, looking and sounding like Alfred Hitchcock. He put the rent check in his pocket, said his Latin Handyman would be by soon to take care of that hot water faucet in the kitchen, and then vanished until August. Haven't seen the handyman yet; perhaps he's coming overland from Ecuador.

The next few days saw an amazing change in the Mistress of the

Manor. Normally she is sweet, calm, reasonable and ethical, all by way of showing me up. But now she became a Leona Helmsley, driven mad by all the possibilities of the place. When I got mad, I called it "nesting." Then she got mad . . .

"I can't help it," she said. "I'm symmetrical."

Her unpacking was swift and wondrous: wire hens, cotton Aunt Jamimas, pointilist paintings, pillow-sacks of potpourri, slightly-chipped crock pots. It was like a domestic version of the Miracle of the Loaves and Fishes. What had crowded four rooms was now crowding seven even more.

All I managed to find of my own things was a longsleeved sweater I bought 37 pounds ago, a booklet describing the medical benefits of a company that fired me three years ago, and a pair of binoculars broken during the move from downtown.

The manor is too big for central air, so we bought a bunch of window units that generate as much cool air as the tailpipe of an F-15. Why build air-conditioners that can't cool one room? Why buy them?

By my count, the manor has 29 doors, each with a minimum of two locks. If I misplace my reading glasses, I feel like Foderic of Thuringia, castlekeep for the Duke of Eberbach, fumbling his way to the secret dungeon.

The next few days were full of new-home fun: two blown fuses, a toilet requiring three complete flushings per visit and a transom that is slightly but unbudgingly open. Then came the "Painting Party."

A good number of the Mistress' friends and relations showed up, and they all staked out rooms. Her son hauled over two mahogany beams to "build a bar in the basement" and said he wanted to paint on one basement wall a mural commemorating a three-day fraternity party he once attended while at L.S.U.

I was too depressed to argue. Before me stood a hallway that runs from Nashville Avenue to Broadway. I had a roller, a brush, and two cans of paint called, so help me, "Robespierre gray."

Some of the Robespierre made it on the walls and ceiling, some made it to my face, hair and feet. One of the Mistress's buddies stuck her head into the hall to say, "I never thought I'd see you painting. It looks funny."

Funny? Some things — if you don't have to deal with them — are funny in ways that are beyond their control: over-ripe fruit, women in beauty parlors, desk-sergeants. This was not one of them.

The only pal of mine who came by was Big Lou. He took one look at me. "Yesterday a peacock, today a feather-duster," he sneered sadly and left.

The Mistress of the Manor came by and saw all the Robespierre on the floor. "Thank God for Latex!" she said cheerfully.

Thank God for LATEX? Thank God for grunion, thank God for Wolfgang Mozart or Oliver Hardy, thank God for polio vaccine or duty-free shopping, but I am certain in my soul He wants no credit for Latex. . . .

I stopped the painting frenzy at the tiny back room that is to be "my" room, and will, I decided, be decorated only by my second-place trophy in the Jefferson Downs Chaplains' Fund golf tournament (scramble rules), a calendar from Santa Anita and the state flag of Alabama. "I can't help it!" I shrieked. "I'm asymmetrical!"

The Mistress of the Manor stood there, in front of her paint-splattered pals. "If you're not going to be happy here, next year when the lease is up, we can move again."

I thought this over and made my suggestion. "Let's all go straight to hell, shall we?" I suggested. You talk mannerly like that when you move Uptown, with a capital "U".

THE SLOW DANCE OF MEMORIES

The news out of that day's newspaper was about this dance studio they'd closed up on Veterans Highway. All week long there were lunchtime jokes about "Learn to *lambada* for $4700 an hour" and "Hell, I'd teach the old broad to dance for half that."

This kind of thing pops up in the papers every year or so. People old in body or spirit sign up for some introductory lessons and then some smooth instructor in suede or chiffon talks them into more lessons and that's when the fledgling dancer's savings account starts to take a real beating. Finally some next-of-kin who sees their inheritance cha-cha'ing away goes to the DA and it's all over.

A 78-year-old widow who lent her instructor $25,000 was quoted as saying, "They had excellent teachers and I was very satisfied." Speaking of the instructor, who skipped to Mexico and conveniently and reportedly passed on to the great Tango Palace in the Sky, the widow inadvertently summed up the whole studio experience: "Who knows when you're going to die?"

In the paper, the studio owner said "Nobody ever made a complaint, they were happy as hell here. They would buy different programs because it saves them money in the long run. Everyone wants to be a good dancer."

Maybe he's right. A few months back — ah, cable! — I caught the National Ballroom Dance Championships on the tube. Two thousand dancers. Little kids in tuxedos and sequined gowns. Old folks, people who had lived for later, saving their dreams for the day the company set them free and now it was here. In-betweens, guys with their hair slicked back with Lucky Tiger, doing the rhumba with Mafia-princess types in diaphanous gowns.

"The U.S. Olympic Committee has now recognized ballroom dancing as a sport," intoned the commentator. "There are now a thousand ballroom dance spots in America, from the Coconut Grove in Santa Cruz to the Medina Ballroom in Minneapolis."

There's one around here, the Jefferson Orleans North, where the people dip and glide, "grace beyond the reach of art." They remind me of my parents.

My parents could dance. When they danced, there seemed to be a new harmony between them, a heightened awareness of where the other wanted to go, the Two and the One, as they went whirling by on gossamer wings and all that.

With dancing, I missed the genetic boat. Besides, when I was coming up, guys who could dance too good were suspect. Usually, there were two kinds of guys who went to dances: guys who could dance good and guys who picked fights with guys who could dance good.

I didn't think all dancers were half-sissy. I mean, I went to the movies and saw Gene Kelly, all big-butt athleticism, slinking around with Cyd Charisse and it put a knot in my stomach. Cyd Charisse! Cool fire in emerald high heels and a hoochy-koo dress and she could keep one foot on the ground and hang the other over your shoulder. . . .

Sure, I'd risk being called a sissy for a couple of turns with Cyd. Only there weren't many girls like her at St. Henry's or Germania Hall. . . .

Of course, it was okay to slow-dance. That was when you slow-ly hopped from one foot to the other and tried to get your hand behind your partner and pull her close enough that the contours of her bustline somehow merged with the contours of your backbone.

The problem was, as it is in everything, picking the right part-ner. I remember a CYO dance at St. Anthony's. I noticed this girl, not bad-looking, standing off to one side with a friend. I watched. Nobody asked her to dance. She was tapping her feet, rubbing her arms. Restrained rhythm. Confined fire.

So when the band struck up the last song of the night, "Good Night Sweetheart," I figured I'd go ask this wallflower for the plea-sure and maybe dance her behind a post and squeeze her like a tube of old toothpaste. Ready for some real cross-gender gratitude, I asked, husky but polite, for the dance.

The wallflower looked at me like I was wearing a three-day-used butcher's apron. "No!" she spat. I was surprised. I had never before seen the human lip curl up that high.

But, ah, when you get lucky with a partner who can dance!

Maybe someone you've only just met, but already she senses your body's uncertainty and knows how to adjust herself to it. You move one way and she's already there. You get gutsy and try something a little fancy and she's there too. And slowly it dawns on you that you'll never step on her feet, that maybe she has no feet. Then you're dancing as well as you'll ever dance and you know the music like you wrote it and you feel like you're jumping out of a perfectly good airplane, making the ninth-inning catch, becoming a butterfly with tireless wings and the universe open before you. I missed out on a partner like that once. I was living in Philadelphia and one night me and some guys went to the Meadowlands to bet some horses. We didn't bet so well. After the races, we stopped for drinks at this place that just came up out of the ground in the Jersey nowhere.

The place had a big dance floor, but we just sat at a table, sippin' n' bitchin'. A young woman came over, pretty but glib and witless as a disc jockey.

One of the guys, older than the rest, had lost the most money tonight and his wife to a doctor last year. Him the young woman asked to dance. "You don't want me, baby," he said. "I'm 54. Almost the speed limit."

But eventually, she got him dancing and she was good enough to make him better. They spun and swooped like Gene and Cyd and when I'd catch a glimpse of his face, he had a smile that peeled his cheeks back to his ears. Far away must have been falsehearted horses and wives. . . .

Deep is grief, yet deeper is delight. To have changed places with him at that moment, I'd even have signed up with one of those skip-the-small-print studios and learned to dance. If they let you pay in easy monthly installments, of course . . .

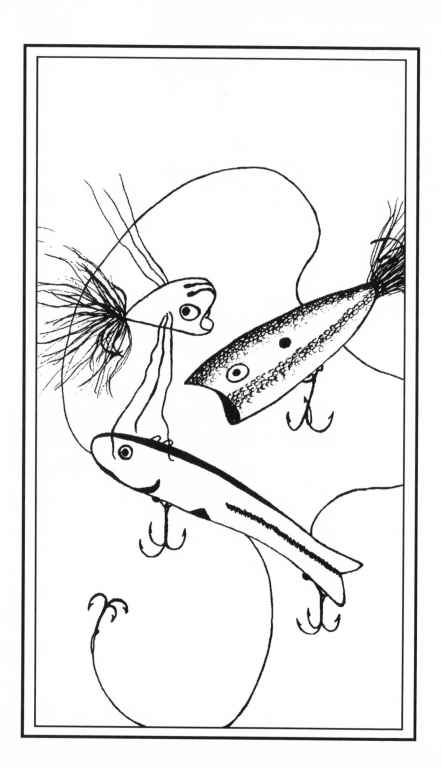

7
Sports

"My hoarse-sounding horn invites thee to the chase, the sport of kings: Image of war, without its guilt."
William Somerville
The Chase (1735)

The state's license plates say "Sportsman's Paradise" and there are few Louisiana utterances more true and succinct. . . .

SPEND A DAY AT THE RACES

The falsely genteel sometimes have a lot to say about racetracks. Most of it is negative and much of it is hard for me to hear.

Because usually the speakers have never seen more of a racetrack than the hard and frantic places where money changes hands.

Just once, preferably in early spring in the South or late spring near the mountains, those people should go to the backstretch, the stable area that is home for horses and the people who attend them. Come on. Take a walk.

Move between the barns to see and hear and smell the stable laundry, wraps and towels and blankets, flapping under the clutch of clothespins in the windy sun.

The early afternoon is best, and on a race day, too. Outside, on the streets and alleys between barns, there's the faint electricity of approaching competition as the summons from the PA system echo softly off pointed roofs. Horses for the next race clipclop out of their sheds and along the streets leading to the paddock, carrying perhaps the finest blanket of the Winged Foot or Black Cat racing stable, a blanket in the finest color of red and black or purple and gold available. The horse wears the blanket like a king is supposed to wear his robes, or at least like a poor man wears a new suit.

Step inside a quiet barn, a place that smells of sweetfeed, liniment and manure. From almost every stall protrudes a curious neck and head, and even the ugliest of them has something, however isolated, of equine grace or mystery. When they hear the faraway bugle or the clang of the starting gate, the horses with the most fire in their blood move to the front of their stalls and stand frozen, ears pricked and muscles twitching. But most of the time, the sounds are usually of indolent snorting, typifying a place at peace with itself.

Then walk over to the rail by the gate where they start the six-furlong races. Maidens, a bunch of young horses that have never won a race, are there, and two or three are acting badly in the gate, heedless of the curses of riders and gate crew. The rider of the eight horse is a young girl, not too pretty, who is riding her first race ever. The gate crew allows her to load last, and has to turn her horse in a couple of small circles before he goes in.

A second later, the gates crash open and from the eight hole in one ragged jump a racing career begins and the exuberance and terror of that moment is time-frozen in the hair-raising and prolonged shout that rips from the throat of America's newest jockey.

And after it is over and she slows her mount to a stop near where she began the race a distant 73 seconds before, the track starter and a steward walk slowly across the track, stop and ask her how it went.

"I beat one horse," she says with a little laugh.

"We were all pulling for you, baby," says the steward, who for once sounds like an official who means what he says.

It's like that at all the good tracks and even at some of the bad tracks on their good days. People spending their lives sharing the wildness and calm of one of the world's great animals.

They say that racetracks around here, even tracks like the Fair Grounds that have been part of this town for 115 years, are in trouble. That the planners and the politicians aren't going to be able to get together and make the troubles go away.

If that happens, I'm going to give the order to round up the usual suspects.

Then I'm going to have them taken out and shot.

RADIO WAS THE OL' REDHEAD

"Remy and Lynn take big leads off first and second, while Nettles holds Burleson close to the bag at third . . . This will be the payoff pitch . . . Rice stands ready at the plate . . . The runners are going . . . HERE COMES THE PITCH!"

I gotta admit right off . . . I've always been in love with the sounds of baseball coming from a radio, Dizzy Dean and Buddy Blattner on Mutual's "Game of the Day," talking about those good hitters in the Giants lineup this year: Don Mueller, Bobby Thompson, Whitey Lockman and this new kid Mays. Madcap Harry Caray faintly yelping over St. Louis' KMOX that Curt Flood had plucked Johnny Callison's fly off the centerfield fence, thereby knocking a certain listener out of a two-team parlay. Lowell Passe's twangy lamentations over the latest misfortune to befall the Houston Colt .45's. Armed Forces Radio bringing the glorious 1967 American League pennant chase all the way to the Republic of Vietnam, and Yaz is winning it almost singlehandedly for those Bosox, hitting clutch home runs and throwing out guys at the plate. And because of hearing it, you suddenly didn't feel as far away from everything as you felt last night.

In the years of my life that I can remember, hundreds of broadcasts like those have woven a thread between past and present for me. They've provided me with reference points for remembering where I was and what I was doing in certain summers.

The summer I visited my aunt in Buffalo must have been 1951, because I listened to Mel Allen do Yankee games and the Yankee outfield was Irv Noren, Gene Woodling and Hank Bauer (Mantle came in '52) and they offered me feelings of a spiritual link with the rest of America when no one in America even knew where the hell I was. (Driving through the cold starry Kentucky night, car heater on and the car radio at full blast — the Cincinnati Reds beating the Cubs and Vada Pinson stretching a single — so that the heater wouldn't make me fall asleep at the wheel. God, people all over the Midwest were listening to this game with me, lying in their warm beds reading magazines and pulling for the Reds. Just like I was. All together at that very moment.)

But all these wonderful dial-a-heroes were not my first loves. Let me tell you about those guys . . .

Their names were the names of gods to me then: Gair Allie, Lenny Yochim, Felipe Montemayor. (How we kids loved to trill that Latin-lilting name over our tongues in exaggerated PA-announcer style.) Unfortunately, Felipe was possibly the laziest outfielder I've ever seen, which is a term of some emphasis because of its redundancy. Like saying that's the tallest Watusi I've ever seen. (Felipe had cunning, though. Every spring when he came north to play beisbol, he was able to convince his wife that she'd have to stay in Mexico City because he'd been unable to obtain a visa for her.) But we thought no ill of Felipe.

The names were more important than the people then. There is a certain age you reach in childhood when it becomes important to seize and remember the names of famous adults, so that you can worm your way into adult conversations when these names come up. And who then was more famous than the Galahads and Robin Hoods who wore the uniforms of the New Orleans Pelicans?

Hearing the sacred names — Dale Long, Moe Panko, Dale Coogan — over those cracked post-war radios with their round illuminated dials was like magic to the kids of the neighborhood, giving them entry to a mystical and powerful kingdom where adults competed against each other and kept score, just like we kids did.

The Camelot of this kingdom, Pelican Stadium, was only a few blocks away from where we lived, on Tulane and Carrollton, and in time we got big enough to go there and sell scorecards. To see the games free!

Until that glorious emancipation, we depended on the wise old story-teller of the kingdom to relate to us via WTPS or WJBW the latest and greatest Pel deeds. That wise story-teller was named Ted Andrews, the radio voice of the New Orleans Pelicans.

In time we would learn to know his name better than all of those whatchamacallims that had played the infield two seasons ago. Some kids knew Ted's voice better than they knew their father's.

His sturdy and distinctive voice became the symbol of continuity for a team that often lacked it on the field — 15 managers in 15 seasons — and when the Pels lost, we took some consolation from Ted's clipped assurance that he would be back on the air tomorrow night at 7:15 when the Atlanta Crackers open a three-game series.

Almost every summer night from 1946 through 1959 you could hear the voice of Ted Andrews carrying news of the Pelicans. You could also hear him fall or winter, doing Tulane football or Loyola basketball maybe, but his was really a voice of summer, a messenger specially suited for the recounting of doubles and double plays.

Now 74 summers young and semi-retired at his home in Avondale, Andrews still has lively mental memoirs of those days.

Such a special messenger needs a special education in both baseball and broadcasting. The baseball part of that education began in Chicago, where Ted Andrews grew up the son of a fervent White Sox fan. As a teenager, Ted vividly remembers seeing the first two games of the infamous 1919 World Series, a memory that became quite painful for the young White Sox fan when it was proved that several Chicago players had conspired with gamblers to fix the Series.

But not all the memories are painful. There are the wonderful memories of baseball divinities like Ty Cobb, Tris Speaker and Walter Johnson. And, of course, Zeus himself: The Babe.

"Babe Ruth saved baseball after the disgrace of the 1919 Series," Ted says emphatically. "I have never seen another baseball player, another athlete, who had the charisma of Babe Ruth.

"I think it was because he always seemed to be able to do anything he set his mind to do. I remember one year Chicago hosted a big international Catholic gathering, a Eucharistic Congress. The papal envoy was at Comiskey Park and before the game Babe went over, knelt, kissed his ring and promised him a home run. Sure enough — BAM! — first time at bat."

But it would take a time before Ted Andrews could wed his love of baseball to his love of broadcasting. After graduating from Northwestern with a speech degree in 1929 ("Played some outfield in college, but like lots of guys, I couldn't hit the curve."), Ted joined a local Chicago station as a staff announcer, but announced ballards, not balks.

"I was the announcer for big-band broadcasts from those great old dance clubs," he said. "You know, the guy who would say, 'And now from the beautiful Aragon Ballroom, the music of the waltz king, Wayne King, and his orchestra.'"

The lure of broadcasting sports finally took Andrews to Oklahoma where he did OU football and Oklahoma City AA baseball. (His successor there was a young unknown from Wyoming named Curt Gowdy).

After Pearl Harbor, he joined the Navy and was conveniently assigned to nearby Norman, Oklahoma. There he met and won a girl named Dot, a secretary from Chicago, and they've been married ever since.

After mustering out of the Navy, the newlyweds headed to New Orleans. Ted's brother had been stationed here during the war and Ted had liked what he saw of the city. He never left it again.

Ted began doing Pelican games in 1946 and was at the mike for the team's shabby City Park finale in 1959. Broadcasting, especially on a minor-league budget, was quite different from what it is today.

"I would travel with the team on the first road trip of the season, to re-acquaint myself with the descriptive details of the various parks in the league and scout the new players," Andrews recalls.

On road trips thereafter, Ted broadcast "live" from a radio booth from places like the Audubon Building or the Cigali Building. As the Pels began play, a teletype operator in Chattanooga or Little Rock would begin to relay a shorthand account of the action. "B10" for example, would translate as "Ball-One-Outside."

Of course, such a cryptic account of a game would be as interesting as hearing someone read a phone book, so Ted used his scouting knowledge of parks and players and a "little acting ability" to vivify broadcasts for New Orleans listeners.

If the ticker said "S2C" — Strike Two Called — Ted, because of his foreknowledge of the habits and eccentricities of pitcher and hitter, could say:

"Brown caught White looking at that slider on the outside corner (Brown liked to keep the ball down and away to left-handed hitters in this park). White looks back at the umpire (White was a crybaby who liked to debate every call), then chokes up two inches on the bat (White always choked up with two strikes)." All that from "S2C" and it made the listener almost feel he was there.

Meanwhile, an engineer in the control booth played a record of crowd noise and when there was a hit or a close play, Ted would signal him to raise the volume accordingly.

It usually worked well, but there were nights like the one when the teletype machine went dead for 32 minutes. "Had to tell the fans that night that we were using a machine and it broke down," Ted says sheepishly.

At home games, Ted always worked alone, which seems odd in these days when there are more people in the Monday Night Baseball booth than there are on the field. Before going to the park, Ted and his wife brought club and individual statistics up to date. As noted, it was a minor-league budget.

Ted chuckles at the memory of how sponsors were handled. "Whenever possible, I tried to work the sponsor's name into the action. Like, 'That was Frank Thomas' 10th home run of the season and he heads for the dugout for the Pause that Refreshes, Coca-Cola.' Nowadays, the FCC would probably get upset."

They would probably also get upset at those little plugs for those advertisers whose sales messages decorated the outfield fences. ("That ball was caught just a few feet away from the Nowak's Slacks sign.")

Once Ted almost made a try for the big leagues. The Philadelphia Phillie radio job was open and Ted was flown up for a three-day interview. He finally decided to turn the job down because in New Orleans he was working year round, doing football and basketball, and such opportunities were not available in Philadelphia.

"The year I turned them down — 1950 — was the year the Whiz Kids won the first Phillie pennant in decades." Ted says with a *Que Sera, Sera* shrug of his shoulders.

But by bypassing Philadelphia, the Ol' Redhead — the nickname was supplied by a station promotion manager — was able to compile his own favorite memories of baseball as it was played in the fading years of the Southern Association.

"The Southern was a pretty good league in those years. There's some pretty fair major league managers — Danny Murtaugh, Earl Weaver, Chuck Tanner and Gene Mauch among others — who learned a lot about managing in the Southern Association."

Although he freely admits rooting for the Pelicans over the air ("I used to say it didn't matter who won as long as it was the Pels"), Andrews hesitates to name a favorite player.

"Stan Wentzel was a big favorite of the fans and a fine, fine centerfielder. Al Flair, a New Orleans boy, was very popular, too.

"There was a shortstop, Gair Allie, who could do it all and had a big future until he broke his leg. Earl Weaver? He couldn't hit beans, but he had lots of spunk like Eddie Stanky. I think he led the league in fielding.

"Pitchers? Even in Double-A ball, you could tell that Vernon Law was pure class and would be a winner in the majors. El Roy Face was a starter here. He looked and dressed like Ozark Ike, but he had talent and oh, was he tough!

"I saw some big home runs out of Pelican Stadium, including some by Harmon Killebrew and Dick Stuart, but the longest ball I ever saw hit there was by a New Orleans native, a guy named Red Lavigne. The fans couldn't really tell how far it went, but in the press box you could see that ball was just starting to rise when it cleared the fence. It must have landed on Ulloa Street."

Though he is semi-retired, Andrews still keeps his hand in it (I'd go crazy if I didn't"), going to spring training in Florida every year to do reports for the Mutual Radio Network. But baseball has changed and broadcasting has changed and the changes don't always suit an old-timer.

"The top ballplayers in the majors are as good as ever, but because of expansion there are now guys on major league rosters who would have had trouble playing in the Southern. With the decline of the minors, some players reach the big time without a sound knowledge of fundamentals.

"And their minds aren't on baseball. In the old days, a reporter could always find players sitting around hotel lobbies or coffee shops, and they would always be talking about baseball. Now you can't find a player anywhere and if you do, they're talking about everything but baseball."

Today's big-name and big-money broadcasters don't rate too high either. "TV has made everybody into 'commentators.' Nobody's an announcer anymore. Now they all sit together and try to top one another's one-liners or ramble on about where they're going to eat and drink after the game. I timed a football broadcast last season and twice they went nearly five minutes without giving the score or the time remaining."

That wouldn't have happened in Ted's booth, he says. He had a big sign with SCORE printed on it placed next to his mike to remind him to give the score clear and often.

"The old-time announcers, guys like Fran Locks of the St. Louis Cards, were thorough in their homework. They got to know the owners and the players, their idiosyncrasies, how they played certain hitters, their superstitions. When there was a rain delay or the home team was losing, 13-3, the announcer had something interesting to talk about." Vin Scully of the Los Angeles Dodgers is Ted's favorite announcer working today.

Andrews believes the dwindling number of minor-league franchises has had a bad effect on the quality of baseball announcing, since there are fewer places for aspirants to gain the needed experience.

"Of course, the minor leagues began to die with the advent of air-conditioning. Why go out to a park and sweat? Then people began to get broadcasts from major league teams. Then came television. People became a different audience after TV came. They came to expect different things from the people covering the games. Different things . . . "

His voice — still pretty sturdy and still sounding like Ted Andrews used to over those Emersons and Sylvanias — trails off and the old man stoops over to pick up his old gray house-cat.

And you can tell by that shake of the head that Ted Andrews is one guy who doesn't believe that "different" always means "better."

P.S. To the Ol' Redhead:

On behalf of all those kids who sat or lay by their radios and thrilled to one of your 1900 or so Pelican broadcasts, a sincere and belated thanks.

CHEATING & FORE-PLAY

To my somewhat cynical mind, the most interesting aspect of golf is the splendid opportunities it offers for cheating.

In the world of sport, there is virtually nothing comparable to the honor system for golfers. If your shot lands directly behind a hackberry tree and no one is looking, you can choose to use the "foot wedge," i.e. a swift soccer-style kick, to move the ball away from the hackberry. And, in golf — let me sound incredulous here — you get to keep your own score! Try to imagine Barry Bonds' batting average if he got to call his own balls and strikes.

It was this tantalizing potential for individual dishonor that sparked my acceptance of Greg Oliver's offer to join the Downtown Irish Marching Club's annual golf tournament at Hidden Oaks in Braithwaite last weekend. No love of golf itself was involved. Golf is like learning to dance a very exact dance, with no margin for personal adjustment, weakness or style. That inhibition and the fact that the first shot I ever hit left the tee at a 32-degree angle and screamed when it smashed into a large pine tree ensured I would thereafter seldom play golf and never love it.

But Greg assured me that I would be playing in a foursome with him, and the play would be "best ball." This means that the foursome always hits shots from the location of the best previous shot by anyone in the group. That is, I could hide my weakness within the strength of the group. He further assured me that there would be ample food, whisky and women on hand — and these are a few of my favorite things. . . .

The preliminaries went swimmingly. A few roast beef sandwiches, a few jars of Salvador's Bottled Margaritas, and a meeting with Tony and Ace, the other members of the foursome. Tony and Ace are older guys, and golf is something that older guys can be good at. I felt bolstered.

That feeling did not survive the first tee. There were about a dozen people on hand, but I could not have been more distracted by a buffalo herd romping across the fairway. I looked down at the ball, which, incredibly, seemed to shrink to marble size.

I gripped my driver like a man holding onto an umbrella in a tropical storm and then swung it like one of Castro's *decamisados* hacking his machete at a field of Cuban cane. The ball never got airborne and, incredibly, now seemed to grow to softball size, which meant it dribbled straight down the fairway about 60 yards. Tony and Ace exchanged glances.

But as we left the first tee, I slipped a couple of extra tees in my left pocket. The rules of golf prohibit using tees off the fairway, and I would not have produced them in view of my teammates. But since I would likely always be hitting last and they would already be climbing back in their carts, perhaps I could improve my fairway shots more than a little by use of this small wooded aid. . . .

As I said, the most interesting thing about the game is its opportunities for individual dishonor.

On the third hole, I hit a pair of shots that caused my companions to take notice. The first was my drive, which I hit hard and stupid and which landed atop the roof of an official's moving golf cart and stayed there. "Park it next to the green," I yelled.

The second was my putt. I putted last, from the fringe next to the green. I hit the ball entirely too hard, but it sped 25 feet — well, maybe 20 feet — directly into the pin and straight down into the hole.

That turned out to be one of only two birdie putts our group could manage all day. Sportswriter Ring Lardner once wrote that the easiest shot in golf is the fourth putt, but Lardner was not with us on the seventh hole. Ace hit a lovely approach shot, which settled like a feather three feet from the hole. All four of us missed the putt, myself putting last and missing the hole by a gibbon's arm length.

We went on, hitting the ball there and thereabouts, hooks and fades, with an occasional good shot to bring smiles back to the group. I almost snuck my tee onto the fairway on the ninth hole, but Ace turned back to encourage my shot, and I had to sheepishly slip it back in my pocket.

The afternoon began to roll along with a sweet rhythm of its own. Smiling women drove by in carts with beer and jambalaya. The course itself was lovely, complete with lily pads and egrets. Of course, I have always loved golf courses, even though I find that far too often you find golfers on them. But today, the camaraderie was as good as the course, and I found myself forgetting the essential lunacy involved in lashing a small ball all over the countryside.

On one of the finishing holes, it happened. Second shot and nobody looking; perfect spot to tee it up for a three iron. Hesitation. Why cheat when you're having fun? The tee stayed in my pocket. The swing, moment of truth, and then the sweet shock of good contact. Suddenly, the others are yelling and the shot I never saw bounds onto the green.

We finished the round at glorious dusk. Our foursome was two-over-par, which wasn't so great. But it was an honest two-over and that felt real nice. Bet some of these guys with better scores didn't have tees in their pockets out on the fairways with nobody looking.

POKER FACES

"Patience, and shuffle the cards."
Miguel de Cervantes, *Don Quixote, II, 23.*

The guy in the long-sleeved gray-knit shirt was going from strength to strength. The last two cards up, a five and a seven, had both been clubs — and that made three clubs showing. He had raised twenty dollars after each of the last two cards had shown.

If you'd asked him the poker players' salutation — "How they running?" — only a half-hour earlier, he likely would have grunted, "Holdin' my own." But now, only a few chips in front of him, down to the cloth as they say, he'd probably say, "They ain't running; they crawling."

So he threw in a chip after the last club showed and only the young Chinese man in the Zima cap raised and he had to call, having the club flush to the king, after all. The young Zima man looked almost apologetic when he turned up his two hole cards, the ace-four of clubs.

"Never disgrace an ace," the man in the gray knit muttered. It was about time to buy more chips or get out of the game. A young guy with a leather jacket and tinted glasses had been sitting behind him quietly for an hour, waiting to get in.

It is the game to be in on at the Flamingo casino. Down on the first deck, away from the tedium of the slots and *touristas*, away from the broads and bells and whistles. Playing a real game. Texas Hold 'Em Poker. A game of imperfect information — only the five hole cards held in common offering information. The rest was watching others move, bet and talk, and from that watching hazarding a guess at everyone's two-hole cards. Not a game of pure skill, like chess, nor pure luck, like slots and roulette. That rare game, that combining of the two antagonists, skill and luck.

By this time of the day, there were only two tables in action in the poker room. This was the serious table. The other table was full of "rocks," conservative percentage players trying to bet a little and win a lot — and everyone knows percentages players die broke. A guy in a business suit, an old black man who never stopped talking, a Eurasian woman in a shabby beret who looked like the kind that walks around her apartment with a yappy dog clutched to her breast.

No, this was the action table and the players had been playing together for hours and most everybody seemed to know everybody else. An old guy, maybe a retired high school shop teacher. Another old guy with enormous ears who played hard and smart. A couple of Chinese. A young guy wearing a Marlins baseball cap over a weak face and a strong mustache. He drank pink drinks with cherries in them and played very loose. And a guy who might have been a brother to the man in gray knit, another man who brought thick, wavy hair and an attitude into late middle age. All guys who'd hopped off the socially approved runways, guys who lack piety and glory in idleness. Weeds in society's garden.

The gray-knit man's beeper went off and he read it and excused himself. He walked over to a public phone, underneath a gold-plated sign that read: "If you think you have a gambling problem, call 1-800-GAMBLER." He got on the phone.

After a few hands, the young guy in the leather jacket began to fidget behind the empty chair. The floorman caught the eye of the player who looked like the missing guy's brother, and he caught a passing waitress and sent her over to the phone to find out if the guy on the phone wanted to hold his seat. She came back and said the guy said he was going to sit out for a while. . . .

The guy in the leather jacket wordlessly moved to the empty chair. He was tall and looked a little too neat, too formal. He looked like he had read all the books on poker.

After a few hands, the guy in the gray knit came back and pulled up a spectator's chair behind the man who looked like his brother. "Know who that was, doncha? I talk to her more now than when we was together. She wants me to talk to Bridget's husband 'cuz he didn't come home Monday night. Why the hell I want to get involved in that? If he ain't hitting on her, what the hell can I tell the boy?"

Then he looked at his Giordano watch, one with cards on the

face of it. He got a waitress to bring him a whiskey and settled in to wait for his chance to get back in the game. A life perfectly compressed from Ace to deuce, four times over.

Poker was played. Everybody took turns winning, only the newcomer got more turns. He caught aces wired on his second deal, he got well on the last card to fill a four flush on the very next hand. A few hands later, he caught the old man bluffing a possible straight and won with queens.

Moreover, he won as if winning was his due, as if he had somehow merited it all, each ace, each spade. He said little, but during a brief delay he snapped, "Whatever we gonna do, let's do it."

Every time the newcomer won, the guy in the gray knit would check his Giordano watch. But what passed now was beyond the measurement of mainstem or quartz. It was nothing less than fortune in its own time and the face of the gray-knit guy was easy to read. It said I should never have gave up on my luck and made the call to find trouble I can't fix. . . .

He kept looking hard at his watch and the newcomer. It was as if he were willing part of himself to be back in that chair he'd surrendered, as if luck sought a place, not a person. Once the newcomer made a raise that nobody called and the gray-knit guy asked to see his hole cards before he threw them in. But the newcomer ignored him, the way a poker book would say to do.

After a while, the newcomer won a hand and the gray-knit guy suggested he hadn't bet in properly. "With those cards, I'd own this boat," he said meanly. But the newcomer just raked in chips and said, "You were in this chair when I got here."

The gray-knit man flushed red. He looked at the Giordano again. It was 20 to 6 and he was a couple of royal flushes away from having even a passable day and, worst of all, some jerk was in his chair and winning . . .

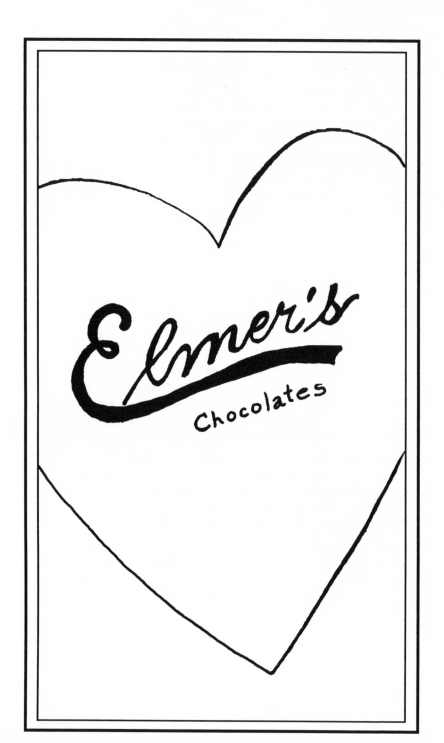

8

Affairs of The Heart

*"L'amour, l'amour fait
tourner le monde."
[It's love, it's love that makes
the world go round.]*
French Song

The most-discussed topic in the history of human speech and we still don't have a permanent definition. Then again, it could be like the time our city's most durable voice was asked for a definition of jazz. "If ya gotta ask, you'll never know," cackled the Dippermouth.

ALL IN THE NAME OF LOVE

The organist crashed in Wagner's Bridal March from "Lohengrin" and the groom and I got up from the first pew and headed for the altar. The bride started up the aisle, looking lovely in her dress with the pearl-encrusted waist. My overriding hope was that my borrowed blue blazer would serve to keep my wings from sight — Cupid's wings, of course.

Me as servant of Eros, messenger of Destiny, maker of matches? Absolutely. Did you perhaps think all Cupids are Rubens curled and cherubic? Here's one that's mustached, flatfooted and ruptured . . .

Admittedly, at the beginning, I had been a reluctant Cupid. After all, in the name of Love, some couples end three decades of companionship with an ice pick or derringer because one of them forgets hair in the face bowl. Estranged husbands have pushed Chevrolets into drainage canals. Estranged wives have thought it over and soon their lawyers were leasing new boathouses at the marina.

All in the name of Love. All this I know, so, believe me, I did not undertake these Cupid duties lightly. Here's how it happened:

A year or so ago, when I was doing a column for one of the city's dailies, I wrote about how, after thirty-odd years, I had looked up Lorena Dureau. When I was a pre-schooler on Iberville Street, Lorena had been my neighbor, a young bride embarking on a career as soprano and music teacher.

When Lorena's husband was at work (I must have instinctively known the rules of being a scoundrel), I would stop by for cookies and a chance to play her piano. "These are the doorbells to the houses of the fairies who live in the piano," she would say. "Now if you bang on them, the fairies will get upset and angry. But if you ring the bells nicely, they will sing for you."

After she moved from Iberville Street, Lorena's life took on a decidedly adventurous tint. She moved to Mexico where for years she sang on national TV and radio. And when she came home, she became an author of several published historical romances.

So in this column, I wrote about Lorena's life and how she had never lost that fairy-tale cast of mind and what a blessing that had been for her and those who know her.

A few days later, I got a phone call. It was an older voice who said he was George Lehleitner and would I "favor" him with Lorena's phone number because his wife had died the year before and Lorena sounded like the woman he'd been looking for to ease his aloneness.

Naturally I refused. This, after all, is a time when all telephone lovers have to do for fulfillment is dial 976-SEEK and be excited or soothed by some fantasy lover at two bucks a minute.

But then George said "If I pledge you my word that I will not bother the lady if she refuses my attentions, will you give me the number?"

I pledge you my word? Mercy, when's the last time in this day and age anyone said that to you and remotely sounded like they meant it? If he'd said "Plight my troth" or "Forsooth, let us not tarry," it could not have sounded more archaic to me.

Okay, I'm a sucker for archaisms. I gave him the phone number and forgot the whole thing.

Then a few months ago, I got another call from George Henry Lehleitner, inviting me to lunch.

Frankly, I'd forgotten the name, but I never forget the exquisite pleasures of a free lunch. So I agreed and on the way to the restaurant discovered George to be an Irish Channel boy who'd made a nice piece of money and now lived across the lake, a gentleman with equal weight on both components of that word.

Surprised as I was to meet a true gentleman, I was even more surprised to find another luncheon companion waiting for me: Lorena, sporting an engagement ring with a stone big enough to knock back the bowler of Diamond Jim Brady.

It turns out George had phoned and Lorena of course had said no as I of course had said no. But she too found George to be a mighty persistent and persuasive sort. And soon Lorena's phone calls to her buddies Lanie Shapiro and Beatrix Krieger were falling off and she was starting to lose weight and getting that twinkle in her eye.

Now she and George were getting married at Trinity Evangelical and because of my role in all this, I had been honored as best man.

And so George and Lorena, two beautiful people who believe in possibilities, have exchanged rings and vows and they are standing at the altar listening to George's daughter singing the "Ave Maria." Both their lips are soundlessly singing along and in their eyes you can see the young part of ourselves, the quick movement never far from our false-faces of age and experience, everready to leap up at love's irresistible knock.

Wait a second; I think I feel my wings growing a bit . . .

WRITINGS ON THE HEART

The overhead fans hung straight down on long poles from botched-yellow beams and turned faithfully, one fast, one slow.

The gray air made by the fans got under and stirred the tablecloths covering the patio's little restaurant tables. The linen tablecloths were clean and exceptionally white.

There was an arch a few yards from his table and just beyond that, the small and exquisite courtyard of the Napoleon House. In the courtyard, the evening breeze had gotten the palm leaves to nuzzle one another. Sometimes they touched the high wall of dampened bricks.

Beyond the wall was an upstairs with a balcony. The sunlight fell with spectacular softness on the balcony. A silvery kind of day, a day that could fly.

It was the perfect place and perfect time for a near-perfect drink: The Pimm's Cup. The first one to be swallowed, the next to be sipped.

The room and the drink were tall and cool, yet there lingered everywhere an imminent heat, ready to move in and take over if the body or mind stirred itself even a bit too much.

The people in this picture were all studies in slowness. They ordered slowly, drank slowly, ate slowly.

The white-shirted waiters all contributed to the feeling of slowness. None looked like he would want to work at a place where the pace was faster. They all lurked around like the shakiest members of a conspiracy.

There were two other men alone at their tables. One wore a tan suit and looked very much like he was waiting for someone. He was a bit past his prime yet seemed to have core enough to still be capable of some things. From time to time, he would get up to look inside the restaurant.

The other lone customer had a Record Ron's shopping bag on the table. He ate his half-muffaletta in sensible bites, without ever looking to the left or right. The first and only time he moved his head was to check his watch and call for the bill. He looked like he lived a life as fidgety as a small bird on the ground, taking tiny bites, tiny steps.

The couples were more interesting to watch. The pair sitting at the farthest table, for instance. She was pale-plain and in the presence of flashier company might have been pinched and quiet. But here and now she was expansive and eloquent, her face flushed with the excitement of her next thought. Her listener was a guy in matching blue shirt and slacks. He was young, but balding and bespectacled and he listened worshipfully to her. He looked like he felt honored to find a woman talking to him and, for the moment at least, seemed totally trusting in the ultimate pleasantness of life.

The other couple looked very *turista*, though not the tentative type. The man wore a significant look, like it was a medal, and he and his companion were waging topical conversation at the highest level, asking and giving no quarter.

At one point, the *turistas* flagged the waiter. He went away looking exasperated as a new-boated fish and returned shortly with a bottle of Pimm's for the customer's examination.

The growing number of drinks helped make this mere people-watching into a reverie, made the tongue tingle, the jawbone numb. Drunkenness, soberly and systematically arrived at, was smoothing out the emptiness of the afternoon. Sip some more and mentally skip stones across the water.

Two young women sauntered in, a bottle blonde, a bottle redhead. Insouciant harlequins, in tight and tired clothes, they looked like street musicians who now hungered to get their act indoors, to play the clubs. They smoked their cigarettes dramatically, told their jokes loudly. They were flip to each other, maybe so nobody got the wrong idea about them. And they were full of the superfluous bravado that suggests deep and true fear.

Then at last the wait of the man in the tan suit was over. She came walking in slowly, dressed in a mint blouse and a suit as clean and white as the tablecloths. Even if you were seeing her for the first time, you felt certain she had seldom looked better.

She sat down and they ordered drinks and antipasto and a cheese board, hearty food with clean, direct flavors. They began to talk and laugh about their separate lives, so it seemed likely they hadn't seen much of each other lately.

After a while, the eating and drinking and chatter slowed and the man said how good she looked. She laughed and returned the compliment and then said how she thought he looked terrific the first time they'd met, at that cocktail party.

"Our timing was always bad," he said suddenly. "You were in love with someone else."

"And you were involved with that woman in your office," she said back. There was no sharp edge to all this; they seemed to truly like one another.

"If I have one regret, it's that we never made love with our minds free of anything else," he said. "I would like to have done that, because I really think we had something of value to give one another."

She then said something funny about what a mess her life had been then and they both laughed reflexively. What writings on the heart will time not erase? Now only the faintest trace of the writing remained and they were trying to laugh about it.

Then the waiter came over and while he totalled the bill, they sat and looked at each other. The look was both sweet and stricken, the truth that their lives had irrevocably missed the connection now shining on them in an amiable yet harrowing path of purity. They left, taking the afternoon with them.

It had been a swell afternoon and it would have been a great place to find a story. Only no story ever showed up, so there was nothing to do now but finish my Pimm's Cup with dignity and completeness.

LOVE'S LAST ACTS

Every morning Elmo Smith loads up the brown Delta tote bag. Today it's tangerines, ginger snaps, Vienna sausages and an ancient .38 caliber revolver. Elmo adjusts his belt, suspenders and thick eyeglasses, and then is ready to go. "She'll like all this when I mash it up," he says brightly. "She ain't got as many teeth as she once had."

It's a gray and blustery day, which looks like it should be cold but isn't. Elmo eases the purple 1975 Chevy away from the front of his home on South Scott Street and heads east.

The drive out to the Lutheran Home on Hayne Boulevard is not without its moments, with the traffic and the fact that on May Day, Elmo will be 95 years old. He talks only of where he is going, not the trouble of getting there.

"I get Maude dresses from Wal-Mart. You know, nice dresses to lie down in. But you know, every time they go out to be cleaned, one of 'em turns up missing."

Years ago, when Elmo Smith started courting Maude Henry, not many who knew them would have figured it to turn out like this. They both had failed marriages and kids behind them, but Maude was in her early 40s, a peppy, redheaded hair-dresser looking forward to the next turn in the road. Elmo was 20 years older, already retired from the Sewerage & Water Board and looking much as he does now. Wits in the family predicted Maude would be getting widow's benefits soon.

That was 31 years ago — and the last couple have been hard on Maude. Diabetes, a stroke, kidney problems. Six months ago, Elmo had to put her in Lutheran. "I couldn't take care of her any more," he says simply. "I fell on my face."

But he goes to see her, to feed and care, a couple of hours every day. He makes a big effort to make a duty sound like a privilege.

He parks the car on the street alongside Lutheran, carefully aligning it with a particular window. "You ever been in one of these places? Man, you'll see sights you won't believe."

But he puts on a nice little smile at the door. Elmo talks a lot, but he would never speak down on anybody and has humor. It's a

142

good commodity to bring here.

Maude is lying down looking at the ceiling when Elmo arrives. She's losing her sight and her skill at sorting things out, but she lights up when Elmo walks in the room. Elmo helps her out of bed and gets her socks, slippers and robe on. Husband helps wife into her wheelchair and they head for the dining room.

The dining room is big, with leftover Christmas decorations clashing with the piped-in music of a Caribbean steel band. At Table 6, Maude takes her usual place between Mrs. Hogan and Mrs. Johnson. There is little talk. Two serving girls are fussing as they lay out the plates, something about 15 minutes of break time. Everyone ignores them.

Lunch is fish, potato salad, carrots and a slab of bread pudding. As Elmo squeezes lemon on the fish and mashes up the potato salad, Maude spots an old woman making her way past the table on mincing limp-steps. "She's crippled one way or the other."

When Elmo is done hand-feeding, he starts telling an old Jefferson Downs story that they both know well. As he tells it, he lays his hand on her arm like a fallen brown leaf. They were arguing that night, the story goes, and an upset Elmo went to the betting window and mistakenly asked for the seven horse instead of the nine. Well, the seven nipped the nine by a head-bob at the wire. "Made you win," Maude finishes the familiar story.

Now it's time for a wheel around the premises. The laws of probability say that these are the final surroundings, the last sights most of the residents will ever see. They are serviceable, but not dazzling. The hallways are marked by crypto-street signs like "Rue Audubon," the banal as adventure.

The hallways are clogged with a wretched armada of wheelchairs, many drivers inching along the walls, hand-over-hand by the siderails. Visitors, no matter how long they've been here, look ready to leave.

Some residents sit in drowsy apathy near the doors of their rooms, their faces craving contact with passersby. Some show only stupification; others smile at being acknowledged, a smile that starts to shrink at the passing of the passerby, the fleetingness of acknowledgement.

All the way along, Elmo leans over to whisper to Maude, waves and calls to other residents. He is a walking bonbon. At last they get to Mrs. McDermott's empty room. Elmo pushes the chair to the window and there Maude can sit and watch the old purple Chevy outside. "Sometimes we go for a ride, get some fried oysters or a Lee's hamburger." Elmo says, but it seems as if this is fairly rare.

Maude says nothing, but there is something good on her face. Who can know the why or how much of the pleasure involved, but it is there, definitely there.

Back in Maude's room, Elmo goes into his tote bag, peels a tangerine, opens the Vienna sausages, prepares it all for after he's gone. Maude coos with appreciation; food plays a big role here.

It's time to go. Elmo and Maude hug, a bit awkwardly, and then he helps her into bed and takes her slippers off and pulls the sheet up to her knees. They kiss like 10-year-olds behind the shed, chins sticking way out, and they hold it a long time. A sweet and haunting kiss.

"Goodbye," he says. Now there are tears nearby. They never come down, but they are there, in eyes and throats. "One day, it'll be goodbye forever," she whimpers. He says nothing, only kisses her again.

Easing the old Chevy into the hurry of Hayne Boulevard, Elmo says, "Hey, I'm gonna help her live, live till the Lord calls. And know what? I think the Lord smiles when He sees what I'm up to."

Ernest Hemingway once wrote that all love stories were tragic, because they all end in the loss of one of the lovers. Maybe it's true that life's curtain fall is always a tragedy.

But if Elmo and Maude are any guides, the final act can have ease and even a quiet joy.

9

Remembrance of Things Past

"The glamour of childish things is upon me, my manhood is cast down in the flood of remembrance, I weep like a child for the past."

D. H. Lawrence
Piano

It's not like draw poker, where nothing that has happened before has any influence on the next deal. In fact, it's the exact opposite. We can only think of things in the past or the future and the past is surer. Or it seems that way most of the time anyway . . .

NOTHING LIKE FRESH SHEETS

The ones you do still see around the city's yards are usually empty, tilted and gnarled.

Once, really not so long ago, they formed a bright necklace around this town, displaying for each passer-by a medley of gaily colored dresses, a throng of socks and blouses jiggling up and down in the wind.

I got to reminiscing about clotheslines the last time I reached into a Laundromat dryer to retrieve my wash from its arid artificial heat. I lifted the bedsheet to my face and inhaled. Nothing.

When people dried their clothes outside in the sun and wind there was a smell and a feel to them. Sleep under a sun-dried, wind-whipped sheet was the secure sleep of a prince, even if your family history was full of shade-tree mechanics and bad-check writers.

Clothes were scrubbed in washtubs on certain days of the week, and children of both sexes were expected to help hang them from clotheslines. This was OK, because you got to handle your old pals, the clothespins.

Clothespins were of two types, the snap kind and the straight or rigid-legged kind. They doubled as playthings. I remember that, for some masochistic reason, we would attach the snap kind to our fingertips or earlobes and see how long it would take them to become bloodless.

On the straight clothespins we would paint faces and use them as soldiers on backyard battlefields. This, of course, was long before Toys R Us.

On days when clothes were hanging, yards were supposed to be off-limits. But if you thought you could get away with it, you played games in which you would run lightly around the yard and let the hanging clothes softly hit you in the face.

Of course, if they were playing away from the house, kids were expected to come back running when they spotted afternoon clouds gathering to "help get the clothes down."

"Where have you been? You saw it was fixing to rain. Now they gonna wrinkle unless you get them hung up in the shed. Well, whataya waiting for? An invitation?"

Of course, in those days, you literally "let it all hang out." Just a glance into a yard could tell you how many of Mr. Canavan's socks had holes in the toes, what Miss Connie's garter belts looked like and the truly enormous size of Mrs. Salvaggio's bloomers.

Once Whitey Ruppert and I watched Mrs. Kaydell's clothesline for days, waiting to "borrow" her sheets and paint them with nail polish so they would resemble "Superman capes." I think Whitey got punished for two years for that one.

The other day, I drove around looking for clothes on clotheslines. I spotted some in a yard at 4620 Spain St. and rang the doorbell. Mr. Jerry Lane came out. He's a widower who retired as clerk of one of the city's municipal courts about a year ago. He lives with his aged mother-in-law and washes clothes a couple of times a week.

"Well, this house was finished in December of 1941, and there just weren't any provisions for clothes dryers then," Lane explained. He said he likes to putter around his yard anyhow; he used to plant mirlitons and the large squashes that the Italians call "cucuzzas" out there, but now "the squirrels eat everything."

"Mrs. Kesberger across the street still hangs clothes; I don't know if she's got a dryer or not. The girl next door has a dryer, but plenty times she still hangs her clothes. I dunno. Outside, towels get fluffier and sheets, man. Sheets are really good.

"Me, I was picking leaves off the sidewalk this morning and I got all sweaty, so I washed some clothes and hung 'em," Lane said. "I put 'em up about 10:30. Now it's 1:30 and I could pick 'em up now. But I'll just let 'em sit in the sun awhile. It's better that way."

THE DAY THE MUSIC MOVED

In a building now full of reluctance, the stack of unclaimed instruments in the third-floor repair shop may be the most reluctant to face the coming move. . . .

The unclaimed instrument, always the symbol of how ill paid one can be to let an ego play in a well-ordered society. These trumpets, saxes and guitars wait, mute and buried, in their chipped and scruffed cases. On each case is tied an orange-and-white ticket reading "Notice: we are moving soon. Please pick up instrument by June 15."

"Everybody here has gotten a personal letter or phone call," said Harold Stubbs. "We're sure reluctant to try to move anybody's instrument."

The tardy musicians can be forgiven a little tardiness in this case. It's almost unthinkable that Werlein's Music would be moving from the store at 605 Canal after 85 years. Harold Stubbs has worked for Werlein's for 53 years and his buddy Nick Mustacchia has been in the instrument repair shop for 40-odd years. In World War Two, when all metals were scarce, they jerry-rigged trombone lyres into saxophone lyres. They find the idea of moving unthinkable.

But in a time when something unthinkable becomes actual every week, it's happening. Werlein's is moving to a store on Veterans Highway, and they'll be taking a whole chunk of the musical life of New Orleans with them when they go. . . .

The original Philip Werlein was a German immigrant who came to New Orleans for a good musical reason. He had first settled in Vicksburg and opened a musical store there in 1842 to service the steamboat trade. He came to New Orleans in 1850 to hear Jenny Lind, "The Swedish Nightingale." Philip liked the city even better than the singing and moved his business here soon after.

Werlein sold and repaired musical instruments and published music, too. "I Have Never Been False to Thee." "Still the Old Home is Best, Mother." Oh yes. A hummable little ditty called "Dixie," in 1859. Was a big regional hit for a while . . .

It wasn't too well-regarded, though, when Yankee gunboats captured the city in 1862. Werlein refused to take an oath of allegiance to the Union, and his property was auctioned off. A loyal employee managed to hide a shipment of pianos in an out-of-the-way warehouse, though, enabling the company to resume business when the war was over.

Reconstruction wasn't good for music sales, but Werlein was an innovative marketer. He organized a rental business and sometimes, "if your family has been deprived of the use of a piano on account of the price of cotton," offered pianos in exchange for cotton, at eight cents a pound.

He sold a lot of those pianos — Erards, Mathusheks, Chickerings, Webers — and when he was gone, his descendants kept selling them, and kept New Orleans moving along musically, too. They brought Enrico Caruso to New Orleans and the great Irish tenor John McCormack, too. They sold sheet music — 10¢, 12.5¢, 18¢ — and arrangements used by most of the city's bands. Kept publishing music, too. In 1890, a big hit was "The Anti-Lottery Polka." Legislators, take notice.

By 1909, they were offering the "Victor Talking Machine" and in the 1920s, that most popular musical gimmick in history, the player piano. During the hard days of the Depression, they sent out salesmen to organize school bands and rent them instruments.

In the early years, the store moved around, from Camp to Common to Baronne and then to several Canal locations, before settling into the Italianate building with the terra-cotta facade at 605 Canal.

No matter where the store was, the business stayed in the hands of the Werlein family, and that kept it personal. A long-time employee got a phone call the other day.

"It was from a woman on Burgundy Street who'd bought one of our first TVs, in the late 1940s, as a Christmas present for her handicapped son. It broke and she recalls Phil Werlein IV driving to her home on Christmas day and lending them his television until theirs could be fixed."

The city's musicians tapped into all this. Louis Armstrong's first cornet came from Werlein's. Fats Domino once ordered — and got — a salmon-pink piano. With red keys. Al Hirt still has all his horns repaired there, too.

In the early 1950s I went to Werlein's with my neighbor Mac. He was renting a guitar and taking lessons on the second floor. After listening to him labor through "Twinkle, Twinkle," I called him a sissy and said he was wasting his time. Mac's last name was Rebennack and now he's called Dr. John and wins Grammy Awards.

Warren Hodgson went to work at Werlein's around that time, and over the years has waited on Papa Celestin, the Marsalis brothers, the Nevilles. He'll miss coffee at Mena's when the store moves to the suburbs, but he'll miss other things, too. It's hard to find the words about what will be lost and why. If you're from around here, you won't need the words.

Hodgson stares out the big window on Canal and outside there are only tourists with cameras around their necks and purple shorts around their buttocks. Not the people to come in to buy music.

Finally a gaggle of freckle-faced kids bursts through the door. They're with a Methodist choir group touring the South. They give the place the once-over and Hodgson asks if he can help.

"Where's Bourbon Street?" the leader wants to know.

WATCHING 'THE SHOW'

I had just sunk flank-deep into one of the plush theater seats of the Galleria 8 and was fiercely contemplating the ultraplastic drink-holder on the seat-arm.

The screen lighted up with the corporate boast: "Sit Back and Enjoy Movies the Way They Were Meant to Be," or some such blather.

When I was light-years younger, we didn't ask, "Are you going to the movies?" We always said, "Are you going to the show?" It was an unconscious distinction, but a valid one. In those postwar years, movies changed three times weekly, not once every three weeks; movies were transitory.

What was permanent was The Show — the neighborhood theater with the delightfully silly name that was never more than a couple of blocks from your home. We went there a lot in those pre-TV days, taking full advantage of the two-bit admissions — a nickel and a Blue Plate Margarine wrapper got you in plenty matinees.

There was the lovely Tivoli on Washington Avenue, The Rivoli on North Broad and the Ashton on Apple Street. There was the Dreamland on Elysian Fields, the Happyland on Burgundy and the Happy Hour on Magazine. "Colored Only" was the sign on the Lincoln, the Clabon and the Carver on Orleans and North Johnson. There were Bells and Beacons, Gaietys and Granadas all over town, at least three dozen or so. Even cow-pasture Metairie had the Aereon and the Patio on Airline Highway.

We kids learned fast to skip those midweek Howard Duff-Ida Lupino flicks and anything with June Allyson. We saved our nickels for those Friday nights and weekend matinees, and got our money's worth. There was the feature, usually John Wayne wading through a wall of Indian or Japanese flesh.

But features were often secondary to the preliminaries: a couple of cartoons, Pathe´ News ("Marshall Plan Saving Europe"), comedy shorts with the Three Stooges or Pete Smith, and serials like Rocket Man, Alan "Rocky" Lane or lion-tamer Clyde Beatty.

My neighborhood offered the Escorial on Banks Street and the

Cortez and the Carrollton. I learned to sneak into the Escorial by walking backwards as others were leaving. Then I could turn my ticket money into licorice whips or Chocolate Babies.

Philip the Cop patrolled the aisles with his flashlight and his enmity to Mother Nature. If Philip caught you with your arm around a girl, you would be ejected and spend the rest of the evening outside with new status. "I got kicked out," you'd tell passers-by, trying to sound like Jimmy Cagney.

What I remember best at the Escorial were the rats. You could track their movements by the rows of people popping up sequentially. Then there was the night of a Tarzan movie when Red Battaglia peeled off his shirt, gave out an Ape Man yell while sprinting down the aisle — and dove into the screen.

The Carrollton was managed by Mr. Peepers, who wore a bow tie and carried an umbrella on sunny days; we knew he was something weird, like a Republican or a Mennonite or something. Mr. Peepers never recovered from the night a guy named Tony dropped three cherry bombs down the commode just as the Germans launched their cinematic attack in "Battleground."

Some of the old theaters survive as auto-parts warehouses or storefront churches. The site of the old Cortez is an empty lot now — amazing how small a lot — with a tiny palm tree growing in the middle, right about where, many Friday nights ago, I dropped a wooly-bear caterpillar on a girl named Dottie in the middle of a Dracula movie . . .

I thought about that little palm tree the other night, sitting in my plush seat at a place that said it was giving me "Movies The Way They Were Meant To Be."

Missing Pontchartrain Beach

Brecht once wrote a poem which contained the line: "The cold of the forests will be with me until I die."

If he had but lived around here, the line would have been about the heat of the swamp and how it becomes a part of those who grow up in it.

On the first Sunday in July, some of us swamp-dwellers went back to a place long our favorite weapon against the heat, a place that was once called Pontchartrain Beach. Somebody got an idea called "Back to the Beach" and charged everybody two bucks to drop by and see what they could remember about the place.

There were plenty of nice things drawn to the lakefront at the foot of Elysian Fields on this Sunday. There were halter tops, watermelon and blueberry snowballs all over the place, and the live music never stopped. The only thing really missing was Pontchartrain Beach.

If I'm not mistaken, the archetypical amusement parks began to be built around the turn of the last century. Up to that time, the only thing the mechanical age had produced, after generations of iron and steam, for the titillation of the common folk was the cuckoo clock.

But now, with working-class leisure time and money to be had, the machine age presented us with the amusement park. Around the country, they carried magic names like Coney Island, Palisades Park and Carousel Gardens — and they invited, dared, demanded, that you check your theories about the littleness or largeness of life at the gate.

The name of the place in New Orleans wasn't mellifluous like Riverview or Dreamland, but it was just as magical in its simplicity. It was simply The Beach. Or, the name of the place, as Chris Kenner used to sing, is "I Like It Like That."

The Beach had everything a great amusement park should have. For much of its existence, admission was free, free to walk barefoot in the sand, swim in a lake that frightened few, smell the roasting peanuts and onions.

It had great rides, too, the ones that challenged speed and centrifugal force, and some like the Wild Maus that scorned centrifugal force. It had the Bug, and the Whip and the Tilt-A-Whirl, and if you tired of those, you could cruise the half-mile Midway and see just about anything.

Like maybe a couple of sailors, packs of Luckies shoved jauntily into the waistbands of their Jack Tar whites, blasting down ducks at the shooting gallery. Or some local show-off, eyes reddened with beer and embarrassment, firing endless baseballs at fuzzy-monkey targets, trying to win that stuffed panda for the girl he just met over near the Log Ride.

And a penny arcade too, with Iron Claws, picture cards of Hopalong Cassidy or Rhonda Fleming, peep shows of Dempsey flooring Tunney or Sally Rand doing things with her fans. And just out the door, a giant clown face with a mouth and red tongue kids could climb in and over till their parents lost all patience.

Then one day the kids had all grown up and their kids had discovered Epcot meant status, Elysian Fields did not. The Beach was sold to a developer in 1983, but his promised condos never materialized.

So now it sits in its own disappearing footprints, waiting for yet another developer with cash and no ideas, or ideas and no cash. It is sad and scarred and a couple of Sundays ago, a lot of people thought it beautiful.

It was a great day for The Beach. Clouds hid the heat. The blue-black of the skies over St. Tammany heightened the bluegreen of the Pontchartrain's water, and gulls looked very white flying across it. Boats lolled just offshore in their pretty show-off way, and hundreds of swimmers ignored the signs proclaiming the lake hazardous. You could close your eyes and let the thunder and pre-rain breeze be the sensations you heard and felt when the Big Zephyr started down that first plunge. . . .

The bands sang "My Girl" and "Sitting on the Dock of the Bay" and those who could remember how the heat of the swamp used to deliver us to this happy place remembered. Congresswoman Lindy Boggs came on stage in a pretty blue-and-white summer dress that the wind kept dancing around her legs and made a nice little speech about getting matching funds from the Feds to serve the lake which had served us so long, so well.

Some of the kids being raised on MTV built walled cities of wet sand or pretended to fish with a hookless string. The lake still has some of its magic; it just needs to be important to somebody. The kids discovering it seemed to be growing aware of new possibilities for the universe, and you couldn't help but wonder where kids can go to be kids these days when cities have no Pontchartrain Beaches.

One ten-year-old girl was having none of it and she kept pulling her dad by the hand toward an exit. "I'm a kid," she said. "This doesn't mean anything to me."

"Tell her it means something to you," a passerby his own age suggested to dad.

"Hey, that's right! It means something to me!"

It was all gone by the 1980s, the experts said, the need for places like this, and then the places were gone, swallowed up by the kiddie theme parks featuring six-foot rodents and Spielberg-like special effects. The experts were at least partly wrong. The places themselves weren't able to survive and they are forever gone.

The need for them is still around . . .

THE VOICE OF SATURDAYS

Sometimes he'd ask listeners to honk their horns in cadence to "Pop-A-Stop-A" and you'd hear horns all over the city, like it was New Year's Eve.

"Dig It" was the title of his theme song, an obscure Joe Houston instrumental that started low and cool and ended with saxophones screeching a wall-warping wail. And over the noise came the voice all us sweet li'l rock 'n' rollers were waiting to hear.

"Time to turn up your radios, little baby-babies and buddy-buddies! . . . Buddy-buddy Mipro! . . . Joyce, Ricky and David! . . . Skim-mild Mamie, Papa Joe and Aunt Ethel! . . . Lookout there, Al Scramuzza! Cow-a-bunga! It's time for the Poppa Stoppa show!"

This was nascent rock, '50s style, long before the British and the philosophers got their parasitic hands on it. There were hip dee-jays out there then — Jack the Cat, Ernie the Whip, Dr. Daddy-O. But when noon Saturday rolled around and you sank into your '54 Merc, pressed your arm against the door so your bicep looked big and wheeled the suicide knob to head for the Old Beach, there was only one voice to take along: Poppa!

His real name was Clarence Hamon and when you saw him live at St. Dominic's or Redemptorist or Germania Hall, he looked more like a Clarence than a Poppa. He was small and soft-spoken, as old as your old man.

But he wasn't like most of our generation's parents, tremblers at the onslaught of rock. He was more like everyone's slightly bawdy uncle, the one who sat at the Christmas table and made fun of adult fears and propriety.

And there was none of that white-throated Eagle Scout rock at the Poppa Stoppa show either, those Pat Boone or Gale Storm imitations of Little Richard. He had access to the North Rampart rhythm-and-blues scene and played stuff that other local stations couldn't be bothered with: soon-to-be-releases by Shirley and Lee, Fats and Frogman, Smiley Lewis and Danny White, Bobby Mitchell and Ernie K-Doe.

It all started at a little underpowered station named WJMR,

operating in a sweatbox on top the Jung Hotel. There weren't many ads sold, so Poppa was sometimes free to put on eight-hour jam sessions without commercial interruptions. or play ribald little classics like "60-Minute Man," "Work with Me, Annie" or "How Come My Dog Don't Bark When You Come Round?"

He was more than a deejay, this nice man who gave free plugs to his friends like Rip Roberts' custom tailoring on Duels Street. Poppa was a lifestyle, and the kids came to see him as much at Lincoln Beach as they did at Pontchartrain.

Talk to him about parental hassles and he'd say, "You think your parents were perfect? Ask your daddy about 746 Baronne Street." You'd think about your old man as a kid, doing wild kid things, and you could laugh and feel better about him.

But rock eats its young and devours its old even faster. WJMR went down the tubes in 1973. Poppa went to a Slidell station and, until 1981, played what had become known as "oldies."

By that time he was divorced and his three kids had scattered, so he came back to the family home on Harmony Street. The tree he planted when he was nine had become what he describes as "the biggest pine in the Garden District." Now in the daytime, he gives away painted pine cones from the tree and hard candies to neighborhood kids he calls "little monsters."

In the evenings, he watches TV in his bedroom, surrounded by Victorian furniture and rock memorabilia. At midnight, he switches on the easy-listening station where an old pal is an announcer and hears all the old rock songs played on violins and harps until he falls asleep.

10
Childhood

"Credulity is the man's weakness,
but the child's strength."
Charles Lamb
Witches and Other Night Fears

Everyone agrees what a great time it is, but when does it end? I think it's the first moment that the child sleeps in the room with a toothless, snoring relative and can make the connection that one day that will be me! If you are one of Destiny's children, that moment doesn't come too soon. . . .

TREASURED SNAPSHOTS

*James Joyce, who wrote many, once said that all stories should begin
"Once upon a time . . ."*
I thought I'd do at least one that way.

Once upon a time, there was a place called New Orleans and a
time when there were few TV sets and even fewer air-conditioners.

The little kids were pacified by "sugar tits," pieces of cloth coat-
ed with sugar or maybe Magnolia milk, and were scrubbed clean
with "wash rags," which the rest of the world identified as face
cloths. When it was time for bed, a lot of the kids couldn't sleep
unless they had a "do-do blanket" in hand.

If they were lucky, they lived in a house with an outside
screened "sleeping porch," and at the right times of the year, they
could come as close to sleeping outdoors as most city kids ever get.

On Saturday mornings, these children, being young, wanted
"to help." Maybe the "icebox" was being defrosted, and you got to
carry the pot of hot water from the "zink" and maybe later get a
spoon and lick up the ice. Or slice a raw potato, coat it with J.O.
Roach Paste and put it by a "roach hole." Or watch your mother at
the ironing board, sprinkling water from a Coke bottle onto the
wrinkled clothes and then ironing them smooth. And at the appro-
priate time, you could plead, "Please don't put no more starch in
mine!"

If you helped, you might get a nickel and you could run to the
store and get a Long Tom or a Stageplank or a Dr. Nut. In front of
the market or the barber shop there were always a klatch of old men
and one might whittle you something, like maybe a whistle out of
a stalk of sugar cane.

Part of the language belonged to you alone. "Cache" was a verb
meaning to hide things under the house you didn't want discovered
by adults: pocketknives and cheesecake calendars were high on the
list. "Razoo" meant everything in sight was up for grabs, and the top
grabber might be called a "dos gris," which was sort of a curse. You
might "pass the post," or sneak-punch, a dos gris, and hope you

connected solidly, or "pee-layed" him.

Play was outdoors and you got so familiar with the insect world that you composed songs and folklore about them. "Lizard, lizard, show us your gizzard!" "Ladybug, ladybug, fly away home/Your house is on fire and your children's alone." Doodlebugs were coerced into a ball and rolled around with twigs. Lightning bugs were caught in a jar and held for nightfall. Wings were plucked from mosquito hawks so they might cling to your finger with vibrating tails.

In daytime, you flew kites with razor blades tied to the tie and tried to slice your neighbor's line. Or you painted clothespins to look like soldiers and fired kitchen matches at each other. Or you shot passing girls with "rubber-band guns" and then fled the scene on your "skate-mobile," a couple of roller skates nailed to boards. Truly bad boys stole the little stack of quarters people would leave on their NOPSI meters to pay weekly premiums to the insurance man.

Some nights someone's dad was in a good mood and he'd pile you in the family Nash or Studebaker for a trip to an ice cream parlor like Melba's on Franklin or Gold Seal on Canal. When you got home, you could gather under a streetlight, and, if someone had a deck of cards, play "Pittypat" or "7.5." Or maybe a good game of "Wireball," tossing and catching a ball over the telephone lines. Or "Hunt the Hay" or "1-2-3 Redlight," until some neighbor would lean out and yell "I know your family! Now go on home or I'll tell 'em when I see 'em!"

And when you got home, you would be examined for mosquito bites and each would be attended by Dr. Tischenor's, the bottle that had the Confederate soldier on the front and contained "the best antiseptic in town."

Once upon a time . . .

FORBIDDEN FRUIT IS SWEET

Already it had been one of those flat-tire, no-spare kind of days. When I drove up in front of my house, it got even less good.

There across the street, two gardeners from Central America were taking a chain saw to my neighbor's Japanese plum tree. One guy was slicing up the limbs so they'd fit in the back of a silver-coated Dodge Ram truck.

I crossed the street and tried to find out why my neighbor had ordered the tree cut down. But since my Spanish is limited to ordering beer and eggs and bossing a burro around, I ended up waving my arms a lot. The gardeners just smiled and gave me one of those, "Yes, we're new to the country, why are you trying to frighten us?" looks.

I finally decided that my neighbor was having the tree carved up because he is an adult.

There are clear lines of demarcation between adults and children. In New Orleans, one of these lines separates attitudes toward Japanese plum trees.

For adults who grow them in their back yards or front lawns, the trees are not for display and the plums are not for eating. They are there only to trick passing children into trespassing, so they can be scolded or shot at. There is a psychological term to describe this particular adult behavior; plum-retentive, I think it's called.

But for kids, who call the trees "Japanee plums," it's different. Only their young eyes can truly appreciate the bright yellow color of a ripe plum. Only their young mouths can truly savor the sweetness — after spitting out a couple of large brown seeds. And only their young memories can set aside the astringent taste of one that wasn't ripe. The unripe ones have another use, though: they are perfect for bombarding classroom enemies when china balls aren't handy.

It is the youthful sense of adventure that most responds to the Japanee plum tree. For many New Orleanians, it is where they learned the pleasures of forbidden fruit.

I remember after-school raids on these forbidden trees, and the hardest to get was naturally the most desired. The tree owners in the main defended their property with oaths, though sometimes they enlisted the aid of dogs, police and broomsticks.

Here are some adult facts about the trees they were protecting, courtesy of Dan Gill of the Louisiana Cooperative Extension Service.

"They're Japanese, but they're not really a plum tree, per se," Gill said. "They're more properly called the loquat. They're out of sync with all the other trees in the area because they flower in the fall, carry their fruit over the winter and ripen in the spring. They're very tropical and only south of Baton Rouge is it consistently warm enough in winter for them to prosper."

Once there were some ripe plums that caught my eye on the way home from school. My companions assured me that the owner didn't mind kids in his trees so long as they didn't break any branches. I had filled three pockets when the reportedly friendly owner arrived, popping a towel at my retreating backside. I ran four blocks before crawling under the steps of a duplex and eating the best plums I ever had in my life.

I thought all those thoughts as I walked over to the Dodge truck and one of the Central American gardeners. My practiced eye told me the plums were full of early summer juiciness. Using sign language, I asked him if I could pick a couple from the tree's fallen branches. He smiled at me, the way one smiles at a madman so as not to upset him. It's OK, his look said, but it had a question mark hanging on the end of it.

I took a big squishy bite. Sure mister, I know we all have to grow up sometime, my look said back to him. Sometime real soon.

A CRAZY KIND OF COURAGE

There's a fine line between guts and stupidity and this kid was walking it.

I was driving on the I-10 service road, nearing the Cleary Avenue overpass, when I saw him. He was in his mid-teens and he was in sharp focus against the crystal sky.

The overpass at Cleary arches some three-tenths of a mile and beneath it cars roar east and west on the interstate. The railings are concrete, maybe eight inches wide across the top, and the kid was balanced on one of them.

I slowed my car, waiting to see him hop down when reason overtook impulse. But his next step was forward, not down. I pulled over to watch.

He hadn't gone far — sliding one tennis-shoed foot forward, pausing, then bringing the back foot up — before I knew he wasn't coming down. He intended walking the length of the overpass. If he could dare to walk, I could dare to watch.

He was thin and his clothes suggested neither a hero nor a madman. He had on a Dodger baseball cap, a blue T-shirt and khaki shorts.

I scanned the overpass for signs of friends. Surely some of his buddies must be nearby to root or to dare, allies to lend courage. Or maybe some ninth-grade girl, hard to impress.

There was no one. The kid in the Dodger cap was doing this to answer questions only he could hear. I tightened my hands around the steering wheel.

When he stopped the first time, he was just about over the service road. I heard myself whispering, "Get down. Get down!"

He didn't. He raised his arms slowly for a few seconds to steady himself, then began inching forward again.

There are those who say that true courage is a parent slogging through a thankless job or a research scientist logging grueling hours on a worthwhile project. They are wrong. What they're praising may be something fine and true, but it's not what Homer had in mind when he outlined his *Iliad.*

"I would define true courage to be a perfect sensibility of the measure of danger and a mental willingness to endure it," Civil War Gen. William Tecumseh Sherman wrote. The kid in the Dodger cap may not have experienced the inner softening we conveniently call wisdom, but surely he knew how final would be a fall to his right. On he went.

The second time he stopped, he was near the crown of the overpass. A multicolored whip of traffic cracked beneath him. He waited a minute, ignoring the hurrying public below. Then he went on, one foot steadily passing the other.

He seemed to be moving faster now, showing off for himself, no other audience. Except me, and I would have no chance later to ask him how or why. I just had to judge him on what I saw.

If I'd passed this kid outside a movie or lounging in a 7-Eleven parking lot, would I have thought him capable of anything resembling inner mastery?

The last time he stopped, he was on the downward slope. Had he begun to wonder if his legs could match his heart much longer? Had Caesar at the Rubicon, Luther at the Diet of Worms, Cortes before the waters of the Tezcuco, overcome such doubts?

Unanswerable. But now, watching him pause, I found myself whispering, "Go on. Go on."

He did and some of the stress I was feeling for him went slack inside me.

Call him goofy, but he was taking brave steps for us all, each one a step over the uncertainties and fears that experience carves on our psyches.

At the end, he hopped down and was gone. You didn't know it, kid, but someone was watching and he salutes you, you young fool.

PAPERBOY TOSSES IT IN

There was a time, dear readers, when I did more than beautify the pages of *The Times-Picayune* for you. There was a time when I put it on your porch.

In that distant age, the newspaper was carried to your homes by boys, not the men who bring it nowadays. The thinking was that newspaper delivery was a fine way to introduce youngsters to the world of business and teach them character and responsibility. Also, kids worked cheap.

Having calculated that I couldn't much enjoy my teen-age years on my $60-a-year allowance, I became a newspaper boy. Because of the ungodly hours, much of the experience is lost to memory, but this is what I recall:

The morning began at 5. I quickly taught myself to sleep-walk the mile to the paper station. I'd walk in the middle of the street and bump into parked cars all the way there.

Breakfast was courtesy of the corner grocery stores that hadn't opened yet. The deliverymen left French bread and doughnuts outside, and sometimes I would leave a quarter or two for payment.

If we paper boys got to the station before the papers, we would wait in the washateria at Banks and Salcedo, drinking root beers and dancing to Ray Charles records on the jukebox. Sometimes we'd go to work straight from a late-night dance and throw the route in suits.

Thursdays and Sundays were the worst, because the papers were huge and we had to stuff them with supplements. This was overseen by Mr. Piazza, the station manager, one of a breed apparently chosen for their records of child abuse. "I know kids," Mr. Piazza liked to say.

I had a monster route, about 1,100 papers, on both sides of Tulane Avenue from Claiborne to Carrollton, The bundled papers were dropped off on various corners by Mr. Piazza and delivered on foot. The only carriers who used bikes were the ones who had the wimpy little routes for the afternoon papers.

We not only had to deliver the papers, we had to get our customers to pay for them. The paper cost 45 cents a week and we had to collect a certain amount before we made a profit. It was by going inside houses to collect that I learned the smell of old people living alone, and the smell of poverty, too. I had quite a few customers in the old Dibert tuberculosis hospital at Claiborne and Tulane; Mr. Piazza made me collect those in advance.

All the paperboys lied to each other about collecting from women who came to the door in negligees.

When papers were late or missing and customers phoned the office to complain, the station manager personally drove out to make the delivery. He charged us 50 cents for each complaint.

I was a pretty fast carrier, but the champ was a little guy named "Gootsa." Being a beer-drinking prodigy, he was often late. But he could load about 75 pounds of papers on his back and, doubled over and on the run, fold and throw without looking. One Sunday morning, he got to the top step of an upstairs apartment before going over backward. It was spectacular.

My last day as a carrier was Feb. 12, 1958, the day it snowed.

I was slicing my numbed fingers to ribbons on the steel bands that bundled the papers when an old lady on her way to Mass stopped and said sweetly, "I don't know how anybody could expect their paper on a day like this."

A lightbulb flashed above my head. I walked to Bayou St. John, tossed the papers in and went home to my warm bed.

A couple of hours later, Mr. Piazza was knocking on my bedroom window, shouting that I owed him for 86 complaints. I opened the window and turned in my collection record book.

"You got no future in newspapers, kid," he snarled at me.

Like he always claimed, Mr. Piazza knew kids.

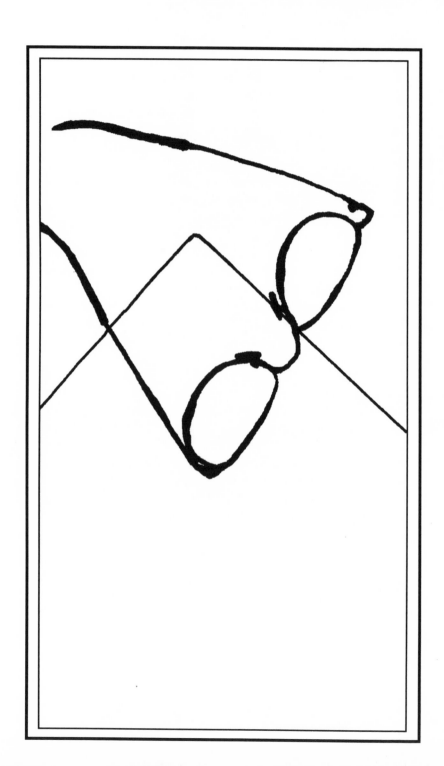

11

Old Age

"I am without politics," he
said. *"I am seventy-six years
old. I have come twelve kilo-
meters now and I think now I
can go no further."*
Ernest Hemingway
Old Man at the Bridge

It's the time we think will surely never
get to us and likewise the time we know
will most certainly get to us. No matter
what the commercials tell us, it is not
Golden Years. The color is more like that
the winter sun paints on the sides of
buildings in the Vieux Carre´, sunlight's
greatest theater. An hour before black
night. A magnificent color . . .

JOY BETWEEN LINES OF AGE

"I wouldn't want to be that old. An old man is a nasty thing."
"Not always. This old man is clean. He drinks without spilling."
Two waiters in Ernest Hemingway's *A Clean, Well-Lighted Place*

The first ones to catch my eye at the Jazzfest were not old. They were very young. They looked like young angels, soft and white, as they made sand castles at the racetrack's edge or ground their faces into snowballs.

Delightful, at first. But after seeing them wince under the hot sun in their strollers or cringe on the shoulders of a half-drunk daddy trying to keep time to the music, you begin to feel like this isn't the best place for young angels. They have no armor as yet against peril and acquiescence.

Old angels are another matter.

Fleeing the midafternoon heat, I ducked into a small tent in the middle of the infield. On a tiny stage were three Cajun fiddlers playing for about 100 people.

On one end sat David Doucet, a fine fiddler, young and serious. At the other end, Dewey Balfa, a finer fiddler, redfaced and jovially reserved.

The show was between these two men.

"This is Emile Benoit, 75 years old," Doucet said of the T-shirted man in the middle. "Yet I go to dances and Emile dances every dance. How come you always dance with the young women, Emile?"

"Well, some young girls like to dance with the older fellas. Some girls don't," Emile said.

He leaned back with the satisfaction of a man who has all the answers he'll need at the moment. He grabbed a lock of his wild gray hair and played at covering a bald spot with it.

Everyone laughed at Emile and he laughed back. You are only a stranger where you feel strange, and it's difficult to imagine Emile a stranger anywhere.

Doucet and Balfa began to play a tune from Newfoundland. Emile got up and did a little jig. Then he sat down and balanced a

Miller beer can on his head. He was a clean old man. He did not spill.

There was a fine, not a bitter, carelessness about all this. Study his old man's face, analyze its twinkle, and you could see the face Emile Benoit wore as a boy. Look as he pokes Doucet in the ribs with his bow. Mischief, my yes, all over the face, certainly. But there too a boyish, long-etched absence of malice. Just as long-held anger can harden on a face, so can its opposite.

Then Emile stopped clowning, laid bow onto string and began to play and sing a song he'd written for a long-ago love. There was a look of roaring joy on his young-old face as his fingers pulled up a profuse past.

An hour later, in the Economy Hall jazz tent, I caught the flight of another old angel.

Red-shoed, wearing too much jewelry, she carried her beer can like a torch as she pranced around and around the edge of the small wooded dance floor. Doc Cheatum's jazz band broke into a snappy "Lady Be Good" and the old lady began to shuffle inside her red shoes.

Her steps and gestures had grown stiff and set, and she danced alone, with no champion or sharer of her dotage in sight. She didn't seem to care. She pursed her lips and hummed to herself through smeared lipstick. People in nearby chairs smiled and took photographs.

Like it or laugh, the old lady seemed to be saying with her body; I have come back to a place of past welcomes, a place most of you haven't the heart for.

It is a scene that could be pathetic, but isn't. The band's clarinetist began to wail on "Poor Butterfly" and the old lady's movements became almost fey as she locked into some near-forgotten spark. She swayed happily, free to make of herself a goddess this afternoon, free to find a piece of coral in the desert of aging.

Young angels can delight; only old ones can teach.

A VISIT FROM A FRIEND

Discarded Christmas trees made the streets a shabby forest and there were few people on them. It was January's winter, the cruel time for young animals and old people . . .

The younger brother Val wasn't young anymore, but he still had charm and a ready smile and they had been serving him well for a long time. They were the parts of the man that came to your mind when you heard his name mentioned, but once in a while when he felt the group conversation was getting along fine without him, you might notice a faraway look on his face, like he was wondering what it was all about or maybe looking all the way to the end of his own future.

Or maybe he was only thinking about his older brother, who was old indeed.

"Old?" repeats Joey to the young black nurse's query. "He saw the Pharaoh's daughter bring Moses out the water. He saw Homer going blind." Joey had heard somebody say that once. He didn't know who Homer was; you can bet on it.

"He's got arthritis all through his body," Val interrupts. "Sometimes he can't get outta bed and put his foot down without screaming. He's seventy-nine."

Joey has come with Val to visit his brother at the hospital again. Outside the room, they mill around, talking to the nurse, mildly hostile and self-conscious, the way workmen behave on college campuses. . . .

They come a lot these dark winter days. Val's brother is in and out of the hospital all the time now. A week in, a month out, a month in, a week out.

"I go to see him almost every day," Val says. "I didn't go the day before yesterday, and he raised hell, telling everybody his brother was deserting him. Yesterday morning I go in early to see him and he runs me out the room. He's just not happy much anymore."

The visitors are worried at the old man's loss of life-interest. They're trying to talk the pretty nurse into getting him to shave.

"Just make up to him," Val urges the slightly dubious nurse.

"He likes you. He likes young women. You play up to him, he'll start to do little things to please you. He won't show it at first, but he'll like it and he'll do little things you want him to. Like shave."

"We do what we can," the nurse says in the institutional imitation of a sweet voice. "But we have so many we are responsible for. Is he your daddy?" she asks Joey.

"No, he's not my daddy. I'm a friend of his. And I want you to be friendly to him, too. Here, take this . . . No, I mean it. Take it. Spread it around then. Buy a coupla pizzas for the whole shift. Don't get mad. Come on. What are you mad for? . . ."

Joey used to be a bellhop at the hotel only a few blocks from here, but he drives a cab now. He likes to come across as this streetwise dude, like maybe he was when he was younger and hopping bells and maybe setting up a politician or two with a girl or maybe jogging down to the liquor store and coming back with a couple of bottles of Old Forester to sell them at hotel prices. But now he is passing deep into middle age and middle class. Now he just gets away with Val once in a while to see a football game or maybe go to Vegas once a year.

Besides, down deep, Joey is too nice a guy to be a real dude.

He just wants to help make it easier now for Val's brother, for as long as he has left and for Val, too. He just isn't real sure how.

They go into the room. Val's brother may be an old man, but he hasn't yet seen whatever it is some old men see that makes them accept things, and his pitiful searching brown eyes roam ceaselessly, begging to be told. . . .

Instead the visitors talk how's-it-going talk and who ate Christmas dinner where and who bet on the Saints. Joey tells a pretty funny story about a guy they all know named Artie, whose mother-in-law had come to visit with her yappy dog. She had tied the dog's leash to a pole in the front yard, but sadly the guy was having some river sand delivered that day and the dump-truck driver hadn't seen the yappy dog, so then there's this hill of river sand with a little leash sticking out. . . .

"So the old lady's a wreck and she makes Artie promise he'll give the dog a dignified burial," says Joey. "So Artie carries the dog to the canal in back of his house, stuffs him in a Glad Bag and tosses him in. 'I gave him a Viking funeral' is what Artie says."

Each time one of the visitors stops talking, Val's brother raises his right arm from his chest and then lowers it. He does it as deliberately as an old lady eating soup in public. He gives no other sign.

Finally, he looks away and Joey makes a sign to Val to step out in the hall.

Outside, Val leans his head back against the wall and shakes it slowly.

"Come on, Val, Come on. You can come back tomorrow. If you want to come back tomorrow, I'll drive you. Come around the restaurant after four o'clock and I'll drive you. . . ."

Val just stands there by the nurse's station, looking down the tiled corridor to the door to his brother's room. You can catch the look on his face and somehow know that he's remembering some minutes that had whirled through his life 60 or 70 years ago, some afternoon when his big brother had let him tag along to the Tom Mix movie — Tom's horse's name was Tony and he remembered him perfectly — or taught him to shoot marbles best when using one of those finger-spreading steelies. That was his big brother then and this is his big brother now and for a painful moment he cannot hide from the fact that he himself is not the same now as he was then.

Joey takes Val softly by the arm and turns him toward the elevators.

"Do what you can," Joey says to the nurse as he presses the elevator button.

OLD FRIENDS REMEMBER

There was just enough Christmas in the little apartment.

A small tree sat like a contented child in one corner of the slender living room. A foot-high plastic Santa wrapped in holly was perched on the lampstand and a step away, in the kitchenette, a couple of thin red candles. Just enough for a place this size, this apartment in the high-rise VOA senior-citizens complex off Read Road.

Trixie Hofstetter was trying to make sure everyone was getting enough turkey and stuffing and lemon icebox pie. "I made it real tart," she promised. "Used three lemons. Sixty-nine cents at Delchamps. Whew!"

Trixie was trying real hard not to be too fussy or gushy about this Christmas occasion, which took place exactly 12 months ago today. But it wasn't easy. Both of her sons, Bill Brant and Paul Hofstetter, were here. In the book of their lives, there were sometimes long passages that didn't include Trixie, but today they were right beside her and calling her "Ma" and she basked in their nearness.

What made it even better was that Hazel "Zazi" Young was here to see it all. On the day when people are drawn to family or people happy to act as family, these two — 82-year-old Trixie and 85-year-old Zazi — had been drawn to one another.

"She's how I got my nickname," Trixie said as she carried away the dishes. "We were shopgirls at D. H. Holmes. I was 16 and she was 19. When it wasn't busy, I'd sneak over to her counter to talk and my boss, Mr. Engle, would come by and say 'Up to your tricks again, huh? There'll soon be a pink slip for you.' So I became Trixie. Sort of an embarrassing name now, at this age."

The boys had brought some whiskey and wine and everyone took a little. "Come and sit down," Trixie said. "Let's all be friends." There was a toast to the day, and Trixie and Zazi began to talk of many things. Trixie talked about her two husbands.

The first had been Frank Brant, a trainer of racehorses, the trainer of Nellie Morse, the only filly to win the Preakness. These were the days when Trixie lived in the Hotel Guyton in Chicago, and once picked seven straight winners at Arlington Park.

The second husband was Paul Hofstetter Sr., a lifelong employee of the Whitney National Bank and an entirely different sort of man.

"He didn't want me at the racetrack, so I'd sneak there and get back home in time to get busy in the kitchen when he came home," Trixie said. "But in those days, ladies wore hats to the track. One day he came home and I was busy cooking all right. Only I'd forgotten to take off my hat. I got caught that time."

Talk turned to Zazi's husband, who was at home. "There's good husbands, only not many," Trixie said. "She's got a good one." Even though Zazi had been a torch singer in her youth and had sung on the radio, her husband never let her go on the road.

"I opened the old Beverly Club," Zazi said.

"Yes, and the main act was supposed to be the blues singer Julia Garrity," Trixie said. "You did so good, she was cussing. Boy, was she mad."

From time to time, others would be permitted on the periphery of the conversation, but not for long. The two old Holmes shopgirls were getting a chance to talk of their time in the world and, except on special days, whoever listened to these things anymore?

Trixie closed her eyes and remembered a poem she'd written when she was 18 and recited at a Christmas party at the home of Holmes' president. It was a long poem about the ultimate failure of riches to satisfy the hungry heart. When she finished, everyone was quiet for a moment and then raised his glass in salute.

Now, Trixie insisted, it was Zazi's turn to perform. "My voice is gone," Zazi kept saying. "For me, for me," Trixie kept answering. Finally Zazi agreed to a duet and they did "Little Red Schoolhouse" together.

Some of the melody got cracked along the way, but there was such joy in their resolve that music seemed to stay in the room after they had stopped singing.

"Remember 'What'll I do?' I heard this girl on TV sing it not long ago and she sang it like you," Trixie said. "It gave me goose bumps. Sing it, please."

Zazi didn't want to, or didn't want to seem to want to. After some pleading, she said she would, but didn't want anyone watching. So Trixie moved her into the kitchenette, behind a wooden room divider. Soon, from behind the divider, came a disembodied voice wrestling with this old supper-club song of aloneness.

"Gone is the romance that was so divine / 'Tis broken and cannot be mended / You must go your way and I must go mine / But now that our love dream has ended."

When Zazi would hesitate on a lyric, Trixie would say it and Zazi would sing it. At the end of each line, Zazi would hold the note with octogenarian tremolo.

"What'll I do when you are far away / and I am blue, what'll I do?"

Outside the window, sunlight was beginning to lose its daily struggle with the dark. Trixie closed her eyes and rubbed her martini glass. Another Christmas had come and was going. Bill and Paul were here and they had eaten and everyone was getting along. Her oldest friend was singing of days that now only exist as secrets of her memory. Everything was fine.

"What'll I do with just a photograph to tell my troubles to? / When I'm alone with only dreams of you that won't come true, what'll I do?"

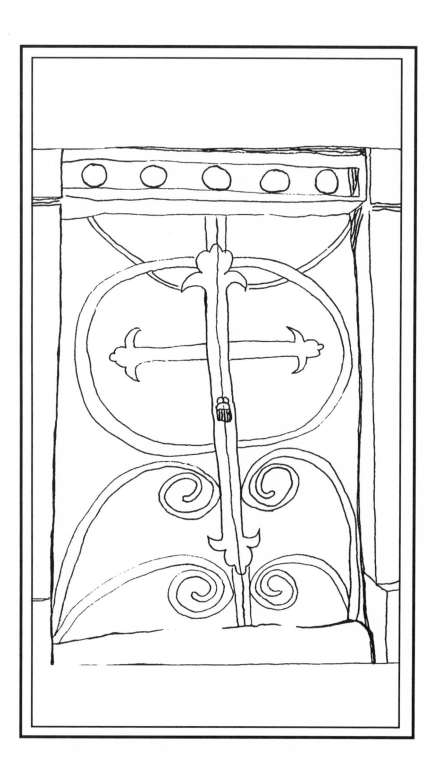

12

Just A Little While To Stay Here

"Death be not proud, though some have called thee Mighty and dreadful, for thou art not so. . . ."

John Donne
Holy Sonnets

It's the title of my favorite hymn/brass-band march and has much resonance in New Orleans. For most of our history, we were an incubator for tropical diseases. Now we eat very well but not very wisely and still depart quicker than the actuarial tables say we should. Yeah, we know death . . .

BLACK CAT'S 'CALL TO POST'

You stand in front of a friend's open casket, maybe a little off to one side, and you look at what's there and you think about your thoughts of that friend. . . .

Listen to everyone talk about what a great guy you were, Allen "Black Cat" LaCombe, now that you're lying here in P.J. McMahon's parlor with your red carnation and your blue tie with the red horses. You're an unlikely saint, the kind most likely to be loved by us sinners in the here and now.

Sure, you made promises you couldn't keep. Remember how Jack Dempsey judged your "Miss Irish Channel" contest and got belted with the umbrella of the runner up's mama? Turns out you had gotten everyone into the contest by promising they'd win.

You never met a traffic ticket you couldn't fix, and you paid back loans with the deliberateness of an old glacier. But you weren't a scanner of life's fine print; for you, everything was in big, bold letters.

On the other side of St. Peter's ledger should sit a thousand charities, small and personal. The keg of root beer for the poor-kid baseball team, the red-beans-and-rice testimonial for the washed-up fighter. Probably your own hard luck made you a sucker for hard-luck stories, even those with a fuzzy side. Remember when you interceded with the judge for the son of the widow with the broken air conditioner? "What's he done?" "Uh . . . possession of heroin, Judge." "Jesus, Allen, I can't do anything with that!" "Yeah, but Judge, the old lady don't see so good anymore, and . . ."

Just yesterday, George Will had a column eulogizing the noted philosopher Sidney Hook. At 85, Hook wrote, "The older I become, the more impressed I am with the role of luck or chance in life." So much for our perceptions of who is truly wise — you were so impressed at the age of 10, when you bet your first racehorse.

Oh, you cursed your luck all right, rang down the thunder from the skies with language you loved the way maybe only a very bright third-grade dropout can love it. "When this hoss gets beat, Cuz, he breaks everybody in the jernt old enough to carry a wallet. But mostly me."

But you never stayed down and you wouldn't let your pals stay down either. Remember your old buddy from the unemployment office, Anthony Arbon? Saw him outside a couple of minutes ago, and he was telling me how you used to tell him whenever he had the blues: "Hey, Cuz. Tomorrow, somethin' good might happen."

The Bible says it's better to light a candle than curse the darkness, but you went the Good Book one better. You lit a thousand candles AND cursed the darkness.

You would have made a great character for the Uncle Remus stories, a loveable critter smart enough to outsmart himself. Take the tale you once told me of getting caught in a gambling raid, and in the Black Maria on the way to the precinct station, you convincing everyone not to give their right names. An hour later, some politico calls the station to get everybody released, only he, naturally, has the right names. So the booking sergeant is calling out, "LaCombe, LaCombe," only you can't answer, since you'd just signed in as "Earl Brown."

It woulda been a helluva wake if they'd all been here. Your old hunting buddy, King Farouk, and your boxing pupil, the Shah of Iran. And deLesseps Morrison, A.J. Leibling, and Richie Della the Paper Seller, who you helped run the biggest floating crap game in the Mediterranean Theatre. And Meyer the Cryer, Leaping Louis, Benny Without a Penny, and Paddy Coco and a million other guys — guys born with a silver spoon, guys who had to swipe plastic spoons and guys whose lives you touched with wit and warmth. But they all beat you to the grave, Cat.

A good, maybe a great, life. Still, a public life. Didn't you ever get tired of being called on for the same stories, the same old charities? Didn't you ever get tired of playing the Black Cat?

Naaaw.

Now it was time to put away thoughts, to try remembering that one day the sense of gain from knowing this guy will be stronger than the sense of loss from losing him. Father Finn said some nice words — that Allen was a guy who made gambling a virtue, and then they put the casket in the hearse and headed for the Fair Grounds.

The brightness of the day only made the sadness a little easier to see. Everybody got out of his car and walked to the finish line.

Across the way, track bugler Wes Mix, looking good in his red coat and white pants, was hoping nobody would notice that he hadn't been able to find his boots. He was wearing black rubber fishing boots.

When everybody got settled, the hearse left the three-quarter pole and started a slow circle around the track. It looked good, a Superior Coach on a Cadillac chassis. There were people waiting at the finish line, whispering jokes about how, with Allen's luck, it'd probably throw a wheel at the eighth pole.

The hearse did sorta blow the last turn and swung wide into the top of the stretch. Along the rail, an old guy with tears in his eyes and an unlit cigar in his mouth started softly snapping his fingers and rooting it home.

"Here comes the winner," the old guy said hoarsely. "Come on Allen. Come on baby. You gonna win this one. . . ."

At the finish line, the hearse stopped. Wes Mix lifted his bugle and, loud and sweet, blew "Taps" and one last time that most wonderful summons a horseplayer ever hears: "Call to Post."

I tell ya, Cuz. Wish you hadda been there. There hardly wasn't a dry eye in the jernt.

THIS WATER HAS CLAIMED SOME LIVES

"Follow me, and I will make you fishers of men."
Matthew, 4:10

The husky cop who had come all the way in from St. Tammany for this, sat in the back of the little aluminum john boat with his hand on the throttle of the 9.9 Johnson. The smaller man in the bow let the hand line play out through his fingers. The boat was going in slow circles.

"Hold it," the man in the bow said. "I've got something here."

The husky cop idled the Johnson and the man in the bow began pulling in line hand over hand. The watchers on both banks got quiet and alert. When the line was in, a long iron rod tied on both ends came out the water, clutching a dripping branch and a rag.

"Dammit," a cop on shore said. The two cops in the boat said nothing and resumed their slow circles.

It was getting late on a winter's afternoon. The sky was the color of dirty wool and the drizzle was patting everyone on the head. On the far shore, many of those watching had opened umbrellas, red and orange and violet.

On the near shore, none of the watchers had umbrellas. From here, you could see what had happened even if nobody had told you. One set of skid marks on the wet grass from where the car had left the street late the night before. A few yards away, another set of skid marks where they had pulled the car out early that morning. There was plenty of glop alongside these marks, the color of mud that lives underwater.

There had been four people in the car when it went, sideways, into the water. Two men and two women. Three had come out of the water.

Around mid-day, they went in to try to get the missing man. First the dogs went in. Somebody had some of the missing man's clothing from home and the dogs sniffed it and then dove into the water.

One dog kept going back to a spot no more than thirty feet

from where the car had gone into the water. But when the rescue teams prodded the area they could find nothing. "There's no current here," one watcher noted as he nodded at the water, moving like coffee stirred once. "He shouldn't be far."

But now the dogs —Golden Labs they looked to be — were standing on shore and shivering. The dogs did not look eager to go back in the water. Their handlers petted them and gave them green tennis balls to chew. The two deputies from St. Tammany were still making slow circles and dragging that rod across the bottom.

A little ways up the bayou all was fine, where Bayou St. John makes an elbow and where it is very nice to watch the waters.

A school bus rolled by, leaving behind an echo of young noise. Passing cars, their headlights on early, slowed and some even pulled over. The drivers got out and stood among the dogs and cops and guys in "Fatality Investigation" windbreakers and latex examination gloves.

The watchers made small talk in low tones. Once in a while, you could hear a chuckle. But most everyone looked suitably tight-lipped, maybe because the family members of the missing man were sitting in police cars a little ways away.

A man in a khaki cap said he was a cousin of the missing man. He said his cousin was 29, but not much else about him. Some things you can help and some you can do nothing about, and knowing the difference puts you in good shape. The man in the khaki cap seemed in good shape.

Somebody mentioned that Bayou St. John is low. "It's about seven feet there," the cousin said. "Man, this little water has claimed some lives."

It was almost five o'clock when the deputy in the bow of the boat felt something. He reached down and a leg came up. He grabbed an ankle and yelled to shore, "Throw out the yellow rope!" The cousin said, "Jesus, he's upside down."

The boat slowly made its way to shore. Several people grabbed hold and pulled the man out of the water, onto the earth out of which we came. His head was back, like he had taken a bad fall forward.

"Step back!" a cop shouted at the watchers. "Get those kids outta here!"

The family got out of the cop cars and moved forward to see. A cop quickly laid a white sheet over the body, but an old woman in a cloth coat had seen enough to know her son was no longer missing, now only dead. "It's him, it's him," she said and turned away.

The dead man lay under the sheet for what seemed a long time. The watchers on the far shore folded up their umbrellas and headed home for supper. Most on the near shore stayed, watching the living tend to the dead.

The cousin went over to talk to whoever it is who keeps records of things like this. When he walked back, he was carrying something. "It's his car phone," the cousin said. "They took it out of his car this morning."

After a while, a representative of the coroner's office arrived, wearing a Yankees cap and carrying a vinyl briefcase. He opened the briefcase and took out a small camera. A policewoman came up with a large camera and flash attachment.

The policewoman walked over and pulled off the sheet with a flourish, like it was spring-cleaning day. The dead man was flat on his stomach, with his arms out from his body and his palms down, like he was getting ready to do a wide push-up.

The cameras clicked and recorded and then another cop turned the body over. The dead man's arms stayed locked wide and now pointed heavenward, like he was trying to keep something from falling on him.

One of the watchers, an old man with a stocking cap and very puffy eyes, said, "God, rigor mortis sets in that fast?"

After some picture taking, they put the white sheet back over the body. A very large cop in a dark jogging suit walked over to two women watchers. The cop knew all about what happened, or at least talked as though he did.

"Some guy drove next to him on Dumaine and said, 'Let's see what you got' and they started racing and he spun out here. And he couldn't swim and grabbed one of the women and she pushed him off and he musta got his hands caught in that soft mud down there.

Well, you wanta go fast . . ."

The two women nodded. They would not be going fast. A tiny drizzle started up again and fell softly on the white sheet. Most of the people and cars were leaving and those still around were now hoping the coroner's truck would hurry up and get there.

No Farewells At Life's End

Old Gentilly Road is a place of auto salvage, welding and incinerating, and then you get to Resthaven Memorial Park, a place for burying.

In the rear of Resthaven, a backhoe claws dispassionately at the slushy ground, churning up wood stumps and chunks of gray-blue clay. Soon the hole will be deep enough to stack two coffins, one on the other.

In the coroner's office van parked a few yards away, Earl McFarland tugs at his Kansas City baseball cap and lights a cigarette. He mentions the smell from the six coffins in back.

"There should be a law, like in California, that all bodies have to be embalmed before burial," McFarland says. "Sometimes we get the undertaking class at Delgado to embalm for us, but that's only when class is in session."

It's a steamy day for burying the unclaimed dead, and the sun shines hard and bright on the tombs and vases and plastic flowers in the main part of the cemetery, a few hundred yards away. But in this little corner, there's only wet grass and mud. No headstones, no markers, no paths. This is Potter's Field for the city of New Orleans.

"Since the economy's got bad, we've done more burying," says John Gagliano of the coroner's office. "We had 46 a couple of years ago and more than 100 last year. It'll be higher this year."

A city carpenter builds the pine boxes for the dead, each one costing about $150. According to Gagliano, most of the dead have families who, because of poverty or anger, refuse to bury them.

Today's six burials include two babies, one stillborn and the other the victim of child abuse, McFarland says. There's also an unidentified man in his 20s, found floating in his underwear near the Old Beach in April, and a pine box simply marked "Tissue."

Keith Harrell and Donald Jackson, two convicts from Parish Prison, are here to do the heavy lifting. They pull on rubber gloves, and Harrell turns up the van radio. It's Dionne Warwick singing "You'll Never Get to Heaven if You Break My Heart."

The FM radio and the backhoe whine are the only noises. The

half-whispered graveside hum of the living is missing, and there are no funeral sobs.

Harrell and Jackson each take an end of the first box and make ready to heave. "Ready-Set-GO!" and it crashes to the bottom, which is already filling with water.

After a box marked "Lloyd Verret" is tossed atop one marked "Kay Lee," the backhoe starts to dig another hole and dumps the mud into the first one.

What about the people in these pine boxes? Him. Was his hair long, his foot light, his eyes once full of promise? Where are the women who loved this man, the brothers to recall some childhood kindness, the friends who brightened when they answered the phone and heard him on the other end?

There's no one at Resthaven this morning who answers for the dead. At least not these dead, who received life's deepest decree with an aloneness that is the stuff of our worst dreams.

The first coffin into the third hole lurches sideways and the top slides off a little, revealing a black bag. "Aw, hell," Jackson grunts. "That was a messed-up body, too."

"At least we sure we burying these dead," Harrell says. "Not like on The Young and Restless."

When the six coffins are in their place, the convicts peel off their gloves and toss them into the last hole. McFarland starts up the van.

"It's not good, but they got to be buried somewhere," he says.

Keith Harrell smiles. He's due to get out of jail on July 9th, and he's hoping to get a job.

"I'll do this kind of work, sure," he says. "These bodies don't bother me. I'll handle any body if somebody pays me for it."

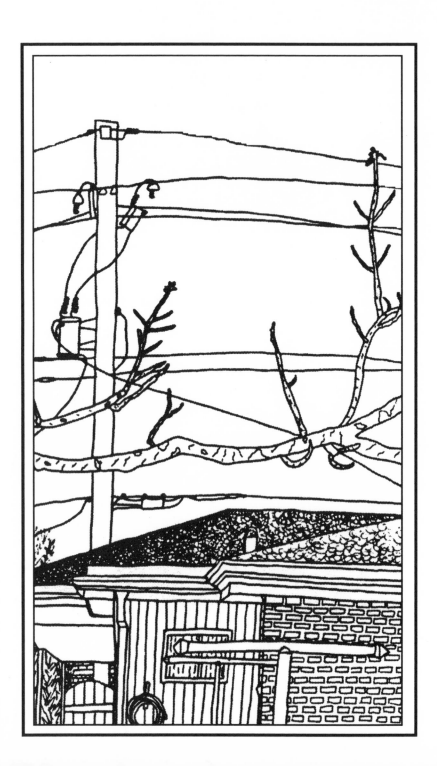

13

Lagniappe

EXTRA — Beyond or more than the usual, stipulated or specified amount or number; additional; more than is necessary.

Oxford English Dictionary

Lagniappe is the piece of pickle pork that the New Orleans grocer throws in when you buy your rice and beans. A little ta-ta, a baker's dozen. This is the something extra of this book; may it not be more than necessary.

LET'S SPEND THE NIGHT TOGETHER

Midweek midnight, over a city shrouded in Lent.

Step into Jimmy's on Willow, three-buck cover, and move to the bar for a tenbit Dixie. Only one stool splits the long bar in half. Along the back of the bar is a long string of pennants, purple-greenyellow, purplegreenyellow, guidons for a Mardi Gras army that has now moved far away. . . .

The stagefront sheet, printed upper left to bottom right, proclaims "Yesterday" and behind it three guitarists pyramid to a pounding drummer, all trying grimly to shake down some joy from the rafters.

A dozen overhead fans swirl dutifully on an equal number of customers. Two girls are hopping around with each other, but the males move to and from conversations with their hands thrust deep in their pockets, like some hillcountry Missourians on the midway.

One guy sits on a plastic chair, and next to him kneels a rumpled young, young chick — Was this girl carded? — seeking absolution from some teenaged sin.

She has to yell over crashing renditions of "Long Cool Woman in a Red Dress," "Get It On" and "Roll Over, Beethoven," and then one of the boys in the band announces a 10-minute break. "Please don't go off, because you may not come back," he pleads, kidding on the square.

The band wanders to the bar. Drummer Paul Haufhausen, Holy Cross '73, gets a coke with some ice and says, "We play Beatles and stuff . . . you know, 'Yesterday.' We usually play around Gentilly. This is our first time here . . . Just not a good night."

The singer comes up and says, "We're gonna cut the next set short. About six songs, I'm losing my voice."

"He's gotta be careful of his voice," Paul says.

The two chicks who've been hopping giggle up to the bar, and one says loudly enough, "These old people could chill out!"

The band moves to the sidewalk. Nobody says anything about the way the gig is going. They point to the busbarn across the street, where streetcars sleep with their doors folded penitently outward, and wonder if in the old days the cars were painted different colors.

The door to Jimmy's opens from the inside, allowing some jukeboxed Mr. Mojo Rising to slip into the lukewarm air. Out steps a long-time swank in a blue-floral shirt, holding hands with the youngest hippie chick in town. Her face is a blank, but the swank's gotta be jovial for what he must do next. . . .

"Hey," he says to the band, "any you guys lend me a buck? For one of them beers in there. Is that what beers cost in there?"

"Jeez," mutters Drummer Paul, digging deep for the dollar. "The band's gotta subsidize its audience."

"Thanks," says the swank, ducking back inside with his hippie in tow. "Keep the faith, baby!"

Later, after all the bars have opened their veins, the last few droplets are trickling. . . .

The lonesome rent-a-cop standing in the parking lot between Shoney's and the St. Charles Tavern is acting very curious about the scene on the neutral ground of Melpomene and the Avenue. Just a couple white chicks sprawled on the grass, smoking and laughing, waiting for the streetcar.

Inside the St. Charles Tavern ("We Never Close"), a sweaty young man is trying to do it all. Freshen glasses at the bar, take orders from the candlelit tables, hop behind the grill to whip up a little omelet, hash browns and chewy biscuits.

At the bar, aging juicehounds, knowing that their remaining nights are all going to be much like this one, drink their Buds with pallid deliberateness. At one end of the bar, a white Rasta and a red-neck are making eyes at the two waitresses from Shoney's. The black waitress is shy and sober, so the white one, the one with the crowded eyes, uses her country accent to order her companion a Coke.

At the other end of the bar, a slender black man waits for a take-out order with an imported beer in his hand and has to listen to the travelogue from the guy next to him: "It's rural. Lotsa trees. No kidding, 25 percent of the state must be state parks. Along the coast, plenty of lobsters . . . I ain't relaxed since I hit New Orleans, know what I mean?"

After two gays get up to leave, the only people at the tables are a big bearded cabbie and a skinny guy with barely enough shoulder to hold up his orange-and-blue Hawaiian shirt.

For a while, they watch the giant TV screen, where Alan Alda is playing George Plimpton playing like a pro football player. Then they start to talk, with the cabbie doing most of the talking.

". . . so Wayne's driving me a thousand miles an hour on the interstate, and this cop comes up next to us. Wayne rolls the window down and says I'm having a heart attack, so we get a police escort to Charity.

"Well, it turns out it ain't the heart at all. It's my esophagus or something, having spasms, and as soon as they give me this green stuff and Maalox, I can feel it relaxing and I can start to breathe again."

"So what the doctors say?" asks the Hawaiian shirt, smearing apple jelly on his biscuit.

"Cut down on the booze. And all the uplift drugs. If I wanna keep living. I don't mind telling ya, I was scared. Man, I was trying to breathe, but I couldn't get no air and it was like some giant had his fist on my heart. I thought I was dying. But I'll say this: I never called for God one time. I ain't no hypocrite. Even J.C. hisself woulda been proud of me for that."

"I dunno," says Hawaiian shirt. "In that spot, I mighta had to pray."

"I'll tell ya. When I was a kid, we made mosta our pocket money selling used coat hangers. But the best day of the year was on Palm Sunday. Me and my brothers usta peddle our bikes over to City Park and we'd peel the trees and go back in front the Church and sell the palms for 15 cents each. But then the church started getting the palms and giving 'em away free. They put us kids outta business. That's when I lost my faith."

They get up and pay the bill and move to the sidewalk. They stand there a couple of minutes. The streetcar comes and the two chicks climb on. A guy walks by, escorted by two stray dogs. A maroon Chrysler Fifth Avenue pulls up to the light, kissing couples front and back.

As the Chrysler pulls off, the cabbie makes a face and says, "They got a lotta nuts out this time of the morning, huh?"

"Yeah," says the Hawaiian shirt, unlocking his bike, climbing on and adjusting his Walkman earphones. "I'll probably see ya tomorrow."

The cab takes off down Melpomene, towards the river. The bike heads towards Dryades Street.

3:20 a.m., in a city shrouded by Lent.

DOG DAYS

In his splendid little book about Earl Long and down-home politics called *The Earl of Louisiana,* A.J. Leibling discovered the toughest elective office in the state.

It must be dogcatcher, concluded Leibling, because every time he asked about a candidate, he was told point-blank that the contender "couldn't get elected dogcatcher in this state."

Sitting on the passenger side on the Cheyenne truck, watching Ron Mitchell watching the gingersnap-colored dog lope along the sidewalk, makes one wonder why anyone, even a politician, would aspire to such a position.

It's been more than 20 minutes since Ron got out of his SPCA truck at the corner of Hammond and Citrus. There were three dogs lying under some hedges there, but Ron wanted the gingersnap dog. He was limping and Ron always goes first for the suffering animal.

But the gingersnap dog had figured things out in a hurry — "It's like they can read the letters right off the truck," says Ron — and was on the move. Ron jumped back in the truck to give chase. The dog, which looked like one of those African hunting dogs, was running with no limp. Up and back the subdivision streets, cutting through the little shopping center on Chef Menteur Highway. Sometimes the dog would look over at the truck with his shiny dark eyes and speed up every time the truck sped up.

For more than 20 minutes. How long and deep runs the bolt of fear. At Read Road, the gingersnap dog got the truck moving one way on a green light, then doubled back and got away.

Ron Mitchell didn't get mad, didn't even curse. He speaks with a reflexive courtesy, with lots of "yessirs," that is by turn charming, annoying and finally endearing. When he grins, you can count his teeth.

"If we had the other truck here, we mighta had him," is all he says of the gingersnap dog.

You need a good temperament to be a dogcatcher these days. Every morning there's a hundred calls asking that an animal be picked up. The SPCA is having money troubles these days, so there are only two trucks available to handle all the calls. It's like trying to keep flies off a roast without using your hands.

For the past six years, Ron has been trying. He comes to the Japonica Street shelter and its thick animal smells every morning, feeds and cleans up the animals already there, then climbs into the Cheyenne and goes looking for more. Like an urbanized *Wild Kingdom* show.

"I really believe in the SPCA," he says simply. "I really believe in what I'm doing."

What he's doing on any particular day can be grim and dizzying. A rattlesnake in Algiers. A wild boar in Press Park. Seventeen roosters from a cockfight on Mandeville Street. A ram who's run on three hooves from Florida Avenue to Chartres and Louisa. A $3,000 parrot in a Lake Vista tree.

"I've only been bitten once," he says with one of those toothy grins. "Yessir."

He turns the truck into a quiet section of Egania Street, checking out a call about a stray. There's an old sofa outside and the stray is hiding under it. Ron gets on his hands and knees and blows the eight-note whistle that people blow to call dogs. The stray sticks her head out from the sofa and Ron talks sweet nothings to her until he can carefully slip a collar over her neck. Once she's out from the sofa, she jumps and licks on Ron.

"She's a pet," he says happily. "Someone'll call for her. Yessir."

He sometimes brings a stray or two home. Right now he has a mixed-terrier named Minnie. When he was married, he found his wife didn't like dogs. "She told me that she or the dog hadda go. So I got rid of the dog, and a little while later, she was gone, too."

Now he's headed for Palmetto Street, stray down the canal. He'll be joined by the SPCA's only other dogcatcher, a newcomer named Lawrence. Lawrence goes down a ways to set up a blocking position. Some Xavier students are nearby, shouting this, suggesting that. Ron slides down into the canal.

The black and brown dog sees him and stands up. How does he know? What ancient melody tells him that Ron is different from the hundreds of other humans he sees every day? No matter. He knows and he turns and begins to lope away.

At their worst, dogs are the underclass of mammalia. At their best, they are day creatures like us, wary and naive like us, allies with us for ten thousand years and still holding up their end of the bargain better than us. It's tough to see one chased by a man and not wish the dog well.

Now the black and brown dog sees Lawrence blocking his way and wheels and heads back at Ron. He runs with controlled speed. Ron gets set with the heavy pole with the net on the end.

When he gets close, the dog shows his teeth, snarls and barks. Then he shifts direction, ducks the net, runs free.

Back in the truck, Ron shakes his head, "If you come back tomorrow, we'll catch him, yessir," he promises. He looks like a TD pass just went off his fingertips.

Another call. On North Rampart, two dogs under a house. Rain is falling in big bullying drops. A man with a diamond earring comes out and says these dogs have been hanging under the house and he's worried they'll knock his gas pipes loose. The man says both dogs are big and he doesn't know if they bite. He says both are strays, but his 10-year-old son keeps calling the female "Koko" and it's clear he knows her. Just another dog who's worn out its welcome. The dog that is a pet at Christmas is a stray by summer.

Ron Mitchell puts on his heavy gloves and takes a long control stick from the truck. There's only about two feet between house and mud and Ron doesn't hesitate. He's down in it and out of sight, whistling, coaxing, hoping one more cornered animal is out of fight.

He gets that male first, then the female. As he lifts her into the truck, the 10-year-old comes over and talks to her through the airholes, softly calling her "Koko."

Ron goes over to the boy and looks him straight in the eye. "Don't worry," he tells the boy. "I'll take care of Koko. Yessir."

If dogcatcher ever does become an elective office, Ron Mitchell is sure of one vote. He'll have mine.

A Visit To The Vietnam Memorial

At the Vietnam Veterans' Memorial, Washington, D.C.

Sitting there for almost an hour, he could get a good reading on how successful Lyndon Johnson and Richard Nixon had been in keeping the war remote from the country fighting it.

He had walked up and down in front of the Memorial for a long time and now had been sitting on a nearby bench. He hadn't connected with anyone yet.

The Memorial seemed to be just another hitching-post on the tourist trail, walk-by for thousands of Americans a week.

An adolescent girl, fat and flushed, collapsed on the bench next to his while her family continued to shuffle toward the Memorial. "Wait, wait," she whined. Nobody turned to look at her.

"Go ahead," she called. "Go ahead, but I'm staying right here and you can't make me go see some dumb wall."

The wall, of course, was ugly, but not dumb, speaking as it does to some 57,000 plucked American roses. The news accounts had warned him that the long-delayed Memorial would lack grace, but it was even more spare and sad than he'd been led to imagine. Fifty yards of black slab, following a low hillock to the point of a "V," then angling off again. Less than a hundred yards total, but big enough to have the names of all 57,000.

He got up and walked back toward the wall.

Here and there, something red-warm among the black-cold slab — an envelope stuck into the wall, typed on the front: "SP/5 John Kittenberg/KIA June 25, 1968/Medal of Honor winner/Comrade in Arms/Friend."

He walked back to the bench and sat down to watch the occasional tourist stop and explore with curious fingers the rollbook that listed every KIA alphabetically and told you on which slab you could find his name inscribed.

Then he saw the tall guy. Even from far off, he could tell he was one. The tall guy would go to certain slabs and look till he found the name he wanted and then pat it, like football players do to each other in huddles.

The tall guy limped badly toward his bench. He looked at him and smiled.

"Did you find everyone?"

The tall one stopped, looked right at him and then managed a weak smile. "No," he said before sitting down on the bench.

"No. There was a young boy named Hunter. I was back at base-camp on light duty, training new meat guys about booby traps, how to enter a vill, stuff like that.

"He went out on a RIF and the first night they put him on an El-pee. The slopes moved past the El-pee that night and he and his brother got the word to move back to the lager and somewhere out there he froze up or got lost.

"He was such new meat that I never got to know his first name, but I thought maybe if I looked in the book I might recognize it. But I didn't."

The tall newcomer said his name was Cleve, from Oregon, and for a while, talking excitedly, they exchanged unit-names and the strange Asian-names of the places they'd fought or been frightened. Neither knew the other's geography or unit, but each at least recognized the names and that was enough.

Cleve seemed happy with the talk. "First time I used words like that in, God-knows-when. Vill, El-pee, lager. You know? Nobody to use 'em with. . . ."

He asked Cleve about the limp.

"Naw. Blister on the foot . . . I went over to the Arlington Cemetery across the river and walked here.

"I thought the Memorial was over there. After 15 years, this goddamn war's still in the wrong place. Looking. That's what we always seemed to be doing. Looking.

"Been getting soft, with a desk job for the last seven or eight years. Took me that long to get settled down." They both seemed to know how long that could take.

In the end, there had been no country to fight for, only guys like Cleve. Because early on, the country had disowned the war and the men they sent to fight it and left them to find their own ways home. Here, at the ugly black slabs, he'd found another one who had managed to do that.

Cleve stood up, and even that little bit of war talk, their verbal breadbreaking over the war, the first he'd heard since — when? 1968? — was over. "I gotta go back to the hotel."

He'd thought about inviting Cleve somewhere for a drink and dinner. But things inside his chest seemed both tight and melting. Things were as always in the presence of these memories, sharp and hostile.

"See ya," he said.

"Bye," said Cleve.

"Yeah. Good seeing you." He meant it.

Truth and heart. In the end, they're the only hard currencies in a world full of paper money.

There was still enough daylight-savings time for him to visit the Washington Monument and the Lincoln Memorial and the other things. But he had no heart for these things now. You couldn't balance those two Americas on the same hot afternoon in Washington.

He caught the Metro back to the hotel and stood under the bathshower for a long, long time.

THIS TOO SHALL PASS

Now that things have settled in the way they have, with promises of civil peace growing fainter or more fantastic by the hour, it is time for the millenarians to come to the fore. They were there to crowd the churches on New Year's Eve, 999 A.D. and 1499 A.D., and our current religionists of the harder-shell variety will doubtless do likewise on the final day of 1999.

These days, millenarians have many proofs of the approaching Rapture, the end-days for a culture that, not being of God, cannot stand. There is plague and devastation throughout, and the spirit of the realm sways under its troubles. Priests butchered near the steps of their churches, police in thrall to other police for their very lives, the honest populace that quivers at the fall of the sun. . . .

If the dream of an improving New Orleans is not dead, it is certainly very sickened.

And history suggests that it was ever so.

No matter what area of contemporary New Orleans you choose to study, no matter how horrific the results, there was an earlier time in the city when things were just as bad. Or even worse.

Worse than, say, the current state of the police department? The one with 38 felony arrests, the piddling pay, the sad-sack morale? Oh my, yes.

In the 1880s, there were less than 100 policemen to cover 150 square miles of city, and they were paid in bonds, which required the services of a broker to turn into cash. Police were usually political appointees and often charged with being drunk on duty. In 1881, Chief of Detectives Thomas Davereaux was killed in a shootout with detective Mike Hennessey. In 1888, Commissioner of Police Patrick Mealy was gunned down by a cop whose police record included 30 arrests in one year.

A prison system tainted by brutality, favoritism and overcrowding? In the 1880s a keeper of Parish Prison was arrested for attempted murder, so it should be no surprise that ill-favored inmates suffered the discomforts of stocks and sweatboxes. But prisoners who could pay for the privilege enjoyed a roomier section of the jail, dubbed the "Orleans Hotel," where they could be visited by caterers and clothing salesmen. There were no police matrons, so women inmates were searched by men and often locked in cells with male criminals. There were no separate facilities for juveniles.

Think gang violence is a modern phenomenon? Try the 1850s Live Oak gang, which carried oaken cudgels and by day hung out under the trees at Elysian Fields and the river. At night, they prowled Gallatin Street in the Quarter, robbing, rolling and sometimes knifing any funseeker they could find. Or how about the slightly-later Shot Tower gang, the Yellow Henry bunch (who specialized in robbing gambling houses) or the Spiders, which bonded at a house on Franklin near Poydras called The Web. When not engaged in their usual criminal mayhem, these stalwart citizens were often employed by politicians to "watch" polling places on election day.

Then, of course, there was the Sicilian-style Matranga Gang, whose riverfront activities drew what they felt was undue attention from Police Chief David Hennessey. For his interest, the chief was slaughtered on the steps of his home — after eating his last meal at Dominick Virgets' oyster saloon on Poydras.

Are you made uneasy by an environment racked by AIDS and lethal drugs? Well, yellow fever invaded New Orleans no less than 39 times between 1796 and 1906, and the death-rate — excluding epidemical fatalities — was double that of New York, Boston or Philadelphia. In 1880, the average life expectancy for a white baby in New Orleans was only 38.1 years. For a black baby, a mere 25.5 years.

Troubled by sleazy statistics on education? In 1900, the city's illiteracy rate was 13.6 percent of the population, double that of New York, triple that of Philadelphia.

Drugs and other mind-bending substances? Until WWI, cocaine and morphine derivatives were over-the-counter purchases. And some of the city's small Chinese population operated a string of opium dens on Common Street between Rampart and Basin, places frequented by both high- and base-born.

Whiskey was always around, of course. On Gallatin or Girod streets between 1830 and 1875, a nickel bought "Irish" whiskey dipped from a barrel of neutral spirits laced with a half-pint of creosote. And denizens of the House of Detention were encouraged to "volunteer" for street work by being given access to such barrels.

The face of race? There were race riots in 1866, 1874 and 1877, including the still-contentious Liberty Monument action. Police pursuit of a black fugitive named Robert Charles led to a 1900 riot that left a dozen dead and two black schools burned. And, of course, the 11 Sicilian immigrants arrested for the murder of Chief Hennessey were lynched or shot dead by a vigilante mob in 1891.

Believe the media to be commercial grubs lying just beneath a criminal topsoil, ready to trade advertising for promoting acceptance of a brutalized world? Henry Hearsey, first editor of the *States*, mysteriously shifted his position on the Louisiana Lottery in 1890, championed the Klan and swapped pistol shots with employees of two rival newspapers. Dominick O'Malley, owner of the *Item*, operated an illegal lottery, was arrested for jury-tampering and went to his grave with 14 bullet wounds in his body from gunfights on city streets. Need I mention a proliferation of guns around town?

All this is not to show a past Golden Age to be gold-leaf. Nor to pour cold water on the notion that our present quality of life is very ill.

Unless you want to hair-split and re-split, too many things are not getting better. But maybe no worse, either. Maybe we can harken to an ancestral memory that knows we have endured this and more before and can again. Maybe we should from time to time cock an ear to the whisperings of history and hear it murmur: This too shall pass.

It's either that or contact a millenarian to reserve a pew for New Year's Eve, 1999, and get a good seat for the Apocalypse.